Phyllida Wilson and ⌐.
of London, and are long-standing friends. When Maxine
returned from South Africa and they reconnected, they
quickly realized that they had both been through acrimonious and very difficult divorces and that they should share
their experiences in a book to help other women facing
divorce. They wanted to write it in a way that offered
real, practical and pragmatic advice on getting through
the process.

521 692 79 6

A WOMAN'S GUIDE TO DIVORCE

Phyllida Wilson and Maxine Pillinger

A How To Book

ROBINSON

ROBINSON

First published in Great Britain 2015 by Robinson

Copyright © Phyllida Wilson and Maxine Pillinger, 2015

The moral right of the authors has been asserted.

ISBN: 978-1-84528-609-5 (B-format paperback)
ISBN: 978-1-84528-610-1 (ebook)

Typeset in Great Britain by SX Composing DTP, Rayleigh, Essex
Printed in Great Britain by CPI Group (UK) Ltd., Croydon, CR0 4YY

Robinson
is an imprint of
Constable & Robinson Ltd
100 Victoria Embankment
London EC4Y 0DY

An Hachette UK Company
www.hachette.co.uk

www.constablerobinson.com

How To Books are published by Constable & Robinson, a part of Little, Brown Book Group. We welcome proposals from authors who have first hand experience of their subjects. Please set out the aims of your book, it's target market and it's suggested contents in an email to Nikki.Read@howtobooks.com

Contents

Preface

Welcome to *A Woman's Guide to Divorce* and may we congratulate you on taking your first and most courageous step into a happier and brighter future as a divorcee!

This guide is a collection of practical, no-frills tips that we have learned the hard way and compiled for women who have already made the life-changing decision to file for divorce. It is not designed to help you to make that decision. You may already have tried marriage counselling or even had a trial separation that did not work. If there is even the remotest seed of hope that you could make your marriage work then we wish you the very best of luck. In other words, if you are still mulling over whether divorce is the route for you then this is not the book for you.

This book is for those women for whom the spectre of divorce has evolved from an intangible and brutal concept into an all-consuming and possibly urgent reality. It is also unquestionably written for those for whom an amicable 'parting of the ways' is simply not an option…

Nor is this book a 'man-bashing' exercise. It is written from our perspective – obviously a female perspective – which may at times give the impression of being biased towards women. This is unequivocally not the case. Some of our very favourite people are men and this in no way reflects upon the male population as a whole. It is what we have learned and absorbed by going through the process ourselves – and we want to share it with you as honestly and as clearly as we can. Our aim is to pass on to you those indispensable things each of us wished we had known before we started on our journey, to help you best manage your divorce process – and to let you know what to expect along the way.

This guide has been written by two best friends who met at university in London. We have walked in your shoes. We believe – and have been told by countless people – that between us, along with friends, colleagues and collaborators, we have notched up a quite extraordinary level of experience; that we have, in effect, 'run the gamut' of experience when it comes to divorce. Our greatest hope is that our hard-won 'enlightenment', which has come over many, many years of struggle, will mean that women may no longer be subjected to unnecessary pain, confusion, grief and unforeseen debt at a time in their lives when they are already intensely vulnerable and living in a state of 'deep fog' (a concept we will return to throughout the book).

Divorce is considered one of the three most stressful events you can experience during your lifetime. And if the process includes having to sell your home – then you are experiencing two out of the three at the same time! Divorce is an emotional learning curve that is often wildly underestimated despite no longer being a rarity.

We want to give you the heads-up on:

- What you should expect and indeed demand from your first meeting with a solicitor
- The court processes

- The most effective ways to communicate with your ex –
  and your solicitor
- How the divorce will affect you, your children, your family
  and friends
- How the divorce is likely to impact on your health, emotions
  and your living arrangements
- And the financial implications of the whole process

We want you to avoid, or at least be prepared for, events that appear 'from left field', whether that is bills, a court summons or simply any situation that you had not conceived of.

Of course, there will always be extraordinary circumstances that no one can predict, but we hope that we have covered the majority of situations you are likely to experience in the process – from choosing a solicitor to post-divorce management In short, we want to empower you to feel – and be – in control of the process of divorce. It is very easy to feel intimidated by lawyers. However, we will show you that as the client you hold the reins: if you are sufficiently aware of the process in the beginning, very little should take you by surprise.

Domestic violence, aggressive residency battles, security and dealings with the police and courts are all included in our 'Extreme Divorce' chapter. We will also introduce you to some 'survival' mechanisms – some tips that worked for us and helped us to cope emotionally and physically through some very difficult and stressful times.

The 'deep fog' is a state that rears its ugly head throughout the whole process. We found we simply did not know where to begin the process once we had made the decision to divorce – just at the very time when we were feeling at our most vulnerable. No one could tell us how to prepare ourselves for our journey to Decree Absolute and how to go about it. If you happen to have googled 'how to divorce', you will have found, just like us, web page upon web page of advertisements for solicitors, conflicting and confusing advice that sometimes flies in the face of common sense and a morass of legal jargon. And boy, is there a lot of legal jargon! We have provided a glossary and some useful websites that will give you a head start.

It seemed extraordinary in an age of self-help that no one has written such a guide before. Our experiences have been intense – and occasionally extreme – and we hope that this guide will help you to avoid some of the pitfalls, explain some of the misconceptions about the divorce process and, most importantly, help you to take care of yourself, your children and your loved ones during the process. It is designed so that you can 'cherry-pick' from the chapters that concern you – and leave the rest – to the rest…We know how incredibly hard it is and we want to help make your experience of divorce the best it can possibly be.

We wish you the best of luck on your journey!

CHAPTER ONE

Preparing to Divorce

'A woman has to live her life or live to repent not having lived it.'

D. H. Lawrence

AN EXPEDITION INTO THE UNKNOWN

It is important to keep in mind that divorce is 'just' a process – 'just' a journey. That is not meant to sound flippant – we simply want to put it into some kind of perspective, because at times it can seem an altogether overwhelming and occasionally 'out-of-body' experience. This journey, however, is completely different from any that you have previously undertaken. It is an expedition into the unknown and you would never set off on an expedition without rigorous research and preparation, would you?

Whatever your circumstances and however good your relationship with your husband once was, this 'expedition' will be devastating. And whilst your personal feelings will differ from the next woman's, there will be an underlying range of similar emotions.

It is particularly important to remember that you are not alone. According to the latest figures from the Office for National Statistics (ONS), there were 117,558 divorces in 2012 (down by 1.7 per cent from 2011). In fact, more than 42 per cent of marriages will end in divorce in the UK and the average marriage lasts just eleven and a half years.

What's more, a surprising 68 per cent of divorces are now instigated by women. So whilst you are going through the 'dark stuff' you may find some comfort in the knowledge that a high percentage of your friends and family will have already got, or will be about to get divorced. Divorce doesn't need to be a lonely pursuit.

But even if you genuinely *believe* that you are prepared for the emotional turmoil, the family upheaval, the very real possibility that you will have to sell your home and the draconian financial constraints that you will almost certainly encounter along the way, it is *always* more stressful and more prolonged than you could ever have anticipated. And that is why in this chapter we are here to help you to prepare: emotionally, mentally, physically and financially. We will give you practical advice along with some tried-and-tested coping mechanisms to help you get through the 'deep fog' state.

GETTING THROUGH THE 'DEEP FOG' STATE

The law in the United Kingdom is based on the premise that one is dealing with individuals who are rational and sane. However, when you are in the initial stages of preparing for divorce you are in a state of 'deep fog'. This means that you and your partner are not as sane and rational as you have been in previous weeks, months or years and the behaviour you both exhibit may be quite out of character because of the state of your relationship. The emotions coursing through you will range from anger, guilt, frustration and pain to sadness, stress and grief – all compounded by bouts of loss of concentration. You now need to accept that you are dealing with emotions of an intensity you have never experienced before and therefore you need to take stock of this state and understand that every decision you make could be impaired or influenced by this set of emotions.

Of course there are varying degrees of acrimonious divorce. We all know couples who have managed to remain lifelong friends and those who have achieved 'do it yourself' divorces because they agree on everything: how assets should be split, contact with children, schooling and any maintenance support. This book is clearly not for them. But the vast majority will end up somewhere on the acrimonious scale – even if the divorce process starts off amicably enough. It is almost as if it is only when the detail is truly entered into that the battle commences for real and the harsh reality of pulling apart a marriage metamorphoses into brutal technicolour.

According to the ONS, during 2011 only 0.1 per cent of divorces were jointly granted to both husband and wife. Of all the decrees granted to one partner (rather than jointly to both), 66 per cent were granted to the wife; in 54 per cent of the cases where the divorce was granted to the wife, the husband's behaviour was the proven factor. Of the divorces granted to the husband, the most common facts proven were the wife's behaviour (36 per cent) and two years' separation with consent (32 per cent).

Whatever the cause of the breakdown of your marriage, it is going to get sticky and painful and you must not underestimate the impact that it will have on you and your family.

According to the American psychologist Dr John Gottman, it is possible to predict with 94 per cent accuracy which couples are destined to divorce. Typically they will display at least one of the following four character traits:

- Contempt
- Criticism
- Defensiveness
- Emotional withdrawal

Contempt is the most significant of these. This predicts early divorcing – an average of 5.6 years after the wedding. Emotional withdrawal predicts later divorcing – an average of 16.2 years after the knot has been tied.

Matrimonial law now rules out any 'blame' attached to the divorcing parties, so the grounds no longer impact on the division of assets, even when the grounds are 'unreasonable behaviour' or one party has had an affair. This is important to bear in mind. This 'liberalization' of divorce, whether rightly or wrongly, is bound to contribute to a rise in the rate of divorce in the long term. New data from the ONS demonstrates that despite a fall in the number of divorces overall, increasing numbers of married couples over the age of sixty are choosing to split up. The greater financial independence of women, the well-documented 'empty nest' syndrome and the fact that there is now less stigma associated with divorce are all reasons that have been quoted for the rise in marriage break-ups in the over-sixties.

One might have thought that age would soothe antagonisms but, surprisingly, older couples are less likely to choose mediation. Indeed, retired couples are more likely to fight over the division of property, perhaps because they have each invested decades of financial and emotional capital in the matrimonial home. In such cases, the couple is more likely to become deeply entrenched in their positions and this can lead to the process becoming more protracted and infinitely more costly.

There is also a rise in prenuptial agreements for those who remarry after having been divorced or widowed in this age group – and this is likely to be because they wish to provide for their own children and grandchildren and avoid the potential for this provision to be 'hijacked' or depleted in favour of their partner's dependants.

MAKING PHYSICAL SEPARATION HAPPEN – THE EGGSHELL PERIOD

The period when you are still cohabiting but have decided to separate can be the most stressful of all and you should prepare yourself for a very unpleasant and uncomfortable time. Both parties will need to come to an agreement very quickly about who moves out of the family home – and when. You will probably both be sleeping in different bedrooms, coming and going at different times of the day and night and creeping around each other as if walking on eggshells.

This time will be painful, traumatic and potentially volatile – so you might as well prepare yourself for this. The good news is that once you have physically separated, you will be able to start rebuilding your life. You simply cannot start to do this while you are still living together. So the quicker you are able to make this happen, the better for all of you – especially if you have children. There will be an overwhelmingly negative atmosphere in the house and this will be communicated to your children even without words or arguments.

If your partner is the one moving out, then he will be taking all his possessions and most probably half of the furniture, too. In the first few weeks after the move, it can be miserable to be living in a house depleted of items of furniture that you have become used to living with – especially if you bought them together or were particularly attached to them. As a priority, do a 'makeover' of your home as quickly as possible – not only for your emotional well-being but particularly for your children. The physical separation is especially traumatic for them and a home with large gaps where furniture used to be can make it very difficult to ignore and move on from.

Every marriage is built on a unique set of dynamics – those idiosyncrasies and peculiarities of relating and communicating with your partner that make up its 'personality'. And that relationship and that communication have now broken down irretrievably. Divorce is no different in that respect. The way in which your divorce progresses will almost entirely depend on the way that you relate to and communicate with your partner, your solicitor, your children, your family and friends and – most importantly – with yourself.

It is vital that the tone of your divorce is set right from the outset – and this can only be achieved by meticulous preparation. Chapter Four is entirely devoted to communication.

FINANCIAL PREPARATION

DO YOUR HOMEWORK

Financial preparation is possibly the most important aspect that you will need to consider when preparing to divorce. If you are a stay-at-home mother to young children it is very easy to get into the habit of allowing your husband to unilaterally control your joint financial situation. He may give you a monthly allowance, for example. This is all very well until the spectre of divorce looms, by which time it is essential to have some idea of the family accounts. You need to know who is responsible for what – so that when you file for divorce you are not going to be caught out and find yourself totally liable for some – or all – of the outgoings (see Chapter Three, 'How to File for Divorce'). If your house is in your sole name you could find yourself responsible for the mortgage despite having no income of your own – and quite possibly the council tax and all the outgoings to boot. If, in a fit of pique, your husband chooses to stop paying money into your account to pay these bills, there is very little that you can do about it later.

It is also important to know as much as possible about your joint assets and financial arrangements and about your husband's assets, savings, pension and life insurance. Make a note of your assets and earnings. Think holistically about what you had at the time you got married, for example: the pension from an old employer or the savings account your grandmother set up for you aged sixteen. Your solicitor will ask you for details later anyway. It is strange how frequently we, as women, although perfectly capable of running all family household matters, including the financial elements, tend to 'revert to type' and let the man deal with financial issues. This comes about primarily when children come into the marriage. This is neither a criticism nor an abdication of responsibility and you should not feel you have let something slip – but now is the time to garner as much information as possible.

Clearly if you are not earning and you and the children are financially dependent on your husband, you are potentially going to find yourself in an extremely difficult situation. That is why it is essential to do your homework and make some provision – if it is possible – or change the current arrangements so that you and your children are not vulnerable. We are not suggesting that all men are heartless cads who will cut you off without a penny as soon as you head for the hills – but a percentage certainly will. And just because you *think* that your husband will behave reasonably when you are divorcing is no guarantee that this will actually happen. You should be aware that the dynamics of a relationship completely change during a divorce and everything will come under the microscope. Men are likely to be more astute and less emotional when it comes to the money side of things, especially if it is *you* that has filed. You too have to become astute.

HIDING THE FAMILY SILVER

If your husband is filing for divorce he may already have started trying to hide some of his assets/savings. In reality, there is very little that you can do to stop this without involving the courts – but you should at least be aware that this may happen. The court has wide powers to retrieve assets that have been disposed of; the difficulty is often proving it. Try to note details of account numbers, endowment and pension policies, etc. Have there been unexplained transfers from any bank or savings accounts? Photograph things like jewellery or any other item that might be easily removed and sold so that you have some evidence of what has gone. Short of appointing a forensic accountant (which is prohibitively expensive), it will be almost impossible to find out such details at a later date.

BANK STUFF

If you are working or are the sole breadwinner then you will need to consider any joint bank accounts, building society accounts and credit cards that you have with your husband. Think about what could happen if your husband decided to try to take ownership of any assets or to use your credit to pay for something that you had not agreed or even to run up a massive overdraft. You will have *no comeback* with your bank or credit card company should this happen.

You can ask your bank or building society to ensure that all credit card and bank or building society payments and cheques require dual signatures. You can also ask to freeze all accounts, however that means neither of you would have access, which is clearly impractical. In the case of joint accounts, if your partner is the main signatory then he can cut off your cards and access to funds overnight. Our experience of this is that when drastic action is taken by a partner in this manner it is either in retaliation for a recent communication or to put pressure on you to agree to something in these initial stages. That is why it is imperative that you try to fully understand and ring-fence your respective liabilities before you decide to file. You may not have the chance later and could end up in the unenviable position of being saddled with vast debts that are not of your making.

Creating a new personal account at the same bank is advisable and easier as they will know you and will potentially already be aware that you are preparing to divorce as a couple. Clearly you are under no obligation to state why you are setting up a new account. If you have had a joint account for many years and you have not been a main signatory then you will have no credit rating – therefore obtaining a credit card may prove more difficult than you think. You will feel slightly affronted by this, probably insulted and angry that, after years of credible credit and as an honest payer of bills, you are now starting all over again. This is another reason to stay with financial institutions who know you and your track record as they are likely to be more supportive. Ask for the same privileges as your partner and do not be intimidated.

It is easy to be given a bad credit rating, which will affect your ability to seek credit for many years to come – even if you have had an impeccable record to date. It seems, and *is*, vastly unfair so if there is any chance at all that you can separate your financial affairs from your husband's *before* you file, we suggest that you make every effort to do so.

Likewise, it is worth exploring who are the guarantors for any loans/hire-purchase agreements that you may jointly have.

When considering the marital home it is worth considering whether it is an asset or a liability during divorce. It is certainly an asset if you are going to sell the property but worthless in preparing for divorce if there is little or no equity in the property – and you should be aware of this.

You should also consider how and where you are going to live after you have filed and whether you could or should consider remortgaging the property.

OTHER POINTS TO CONSIDER

- Pension sharing
- Life assurance policies to be rewritten/trusts, etc.
- Stocks and shares to be reviewed where in joint names
- Investment bonds and other investment plans, policies and trusts to be reviewed
- Life assurance cover to be taken out on ex-spouse where alimony involved (Lloyds of London and others will consider life policies to be taken out on reluctant ex-spouses).

WRITING A WILL

One of the things that any good solicitor will advise you to do when you file for divorce is to make a will if you have not already done so. Any existing will becomes null and void upon divorce. We would suggest that you do this *prior* to filing for divorce so that should anything happen to you during the separation/divorce process, your children will be provided for and your assets will not go to your husband – or his family. This is also a good way of relieving some of the emotional pressure and worry that you will feel about future provision.

PROVIDING FOR GUARDIANSHIP

Equally, it is *essential* that you make provision for who is going to look after your children before you divorce. This is, for obvious reasons, so that if anything happens to you the children do not automatically go to your husband – especially if he has a personality disorder/has been violent (See Chapter Five, 'Extreme Divorce') or is considered unfit to be in charge of your children.

EMOTIONAL PREPARATION

During the divorce process you are likely to be under a level of emotional pressure that you have never experienced before. Be kind to yourself. This means not expecting too much of yourself emotionally. If you are a mother and are working, enormous demands are already being made upon you by your children and your colleagues. If you care for an elderly parent too, it is likely that you are already *in extremis* before you even begin.

Getting divorced is not unlike bereavement and you should expect your feelings to vacillate wildly just as they do when someone close to you dies. Whatever the situation, the man that you married no longer exists and you have quite feasibly lost the former love of your life, the father to your children and your best friend. That is no small loss. It is bound to have a very profound effect on your emotional well-being.

NO SNAP DECISIONS

This period of preparation is not a time to make snap decisions. It really is all about assimilation and review, so if you are being pressurized by your partner or others to get a solicitor or 'go down the mediation route' – resist. Ensure you evaluate and revaluate…and evaluate again.

UNDERSTANDING THE BEREAVEMENT CURVE

Research shows there is a 'bereavement curve', which commonly comprises five very different but often overlapping emotions. You may not experience them all, but the following is a good indication of the range of emotions you can expect to experience:

1 DENIAL

'This can't be happening to me. I'll just bury my head in the sand and hope it gets better…'

Immediately following separation or the realization that divorce is inevitable – even if the decision is ultimately ours – we may be numb with shock, to such an extent that the intensity of the emotions we are feeling appears somewhat reduced. This is quite normal. The inevitable wave of emotion that eventually arrives is also commonly delayed, also known as the 'deep fog' state we referred to earlier. Some people don't feel their emotions for weeks, months or even years in extreme cases.

2 ANGER

'I can't believe this is happening to me – why me? What have I done to deserve this? It's not fair.'

It is quite normal to feel a deep sense of injustice – even when it is *you* who is the one wanting to break up the marriage. Your partner may have been having an affair, been secretly gambling or running up huge debts. He may have been controlling or violent – he may even have been suffering from a personality disorder. It may have been *you* that was having an affair and the process made you realize that your marriage was dead or that you wanted to be with someone else. You may simply have fallen out of love. Whatever the situation, you are likely to feel very angry indeed – especially if there are children involved who are going to suffer as a result of the break-up.

3 GUILT

'If only I hadn't focused so much on my career/the children/let myself go/been so high-maintenance/too quiet/too loud/too weak/too strong/not supportive enough/a total doormat/not attractive enough/too flirty with his friends – we might still be in love and still together...'

You may question yourself about signs that you have seen and then blame yourself for having been blind. Perhaps you *did* know that something was very wrong but pretended to yourself that nothing was amiss. This is a very female trait! Women are very good at taking the blame for everything and it is important that you do not beat yourself up or take more than your fair share of responsibility for the break-up. In most cases a portion of blame sits with both parties.

Bargaining with yourself can play a big part when your divorce is inevitable. You may become unaccountably superstitious or bargain with 'the gods' that if only life can go back to the way it was that you will be a better person/give up smoking/take-aways/go to the gym three times a week. You may castigate yourself for not doing more or imagine that things would have worked out for any number of irrational reasons – if only you had behaved differently. It is essential to move beyond this stage if you are to reach the point of acceptance, otherwise you will be burdened with a sense of remorse and self-reproach that is intolerable and will radically delay your emotional recovery.

4 DEPRESSION

'I can't see the point in anything. I cannot bear to be on my own. Life is not worth living. I might as well give up.'

Depression post-separation is perfectly normal. You are grieving for the loss of the man you once loved (or may still love), your lifestyle or your friends and family (who will inevitably take sides). You may become completely disinterested in normal life – such as watching the news, documentaries, reading newspapers, going to the cinema or socializing – anything, in fact, that involves the outside world. This is because your inner world is taking centre stage and there is literally not enough of you to deal with any extraneous demands on your time and emotions.

You may eat more or less than normal. You may start to drink more alcohol or smoke more – or even take it up again. You may generally lack concentration and may find yourself crying at the most insignificant, random events or things. We both know people who have literally taken to their beds for months, emerging only to eat or go to the pub where they can drown their sorrows – but they have not been parents, admittedly, and have not had to look after children. We can also remember 'zoning out' on occasion because our reality was too painful to bear – or 'tuning out' non-essential details. (See note on PTSD in Chapter Five, 'Extreme Divorce'.) To this day, many years on from our divorces, there are still snippets of news or events that took place in our lives or the world at large that one or other of us cannot recall. For example, one of us during the aftermath of the sale of the matrimonial home sent a chest of drawers to be housed with a family member – and then totally forgot that she had done it.

When you are on 'over-load' it is easy to forget the simplest of things. You are multi-tasking at an extraordinary level with the volume of things you have to do and think about. Your brain is self-selecting and prioritizing. Through all this you will also have to put on a brave face for work colleagues, friends and especially for your children. This is a strain but necessary. The reason it is necessary may appear obvious when things are routine but when change happens on a large or even surreal scale it is important that you are able to compartmentalize your emotions – only sharing as and when you are feeling ready to do so. Your children need to be protected.

5 ACCEPTANCE

'I know that life will be hard and very different on my own but I can see the light at the end of the tunnel and I know that I can find happiness and love again.'

Just because you finally reach the state of acceptance, it does not mean that you will not experience any of the other bereavement-curve emotions again. You may vacillate between anger and sadness for months or even years and then lapse and re-lapse regularly.

KNOWING WHEN IT'S TIME TO ASK FOR HELP

We would always recommend that you visit your GP and he or she may arrange for you to take a simple test, like the PHQ (Patient Health Questionnaire) or the Goldberg Questionnaire, to name but two. Either of these will instantly gauge your emotional well-being. Questions include the amount of sleep you are having, your appetite, your interest in seeing friends and family and even how slowly you are moving, compared to what is 'normal' for you. Depending on your score, your GP may want to discuss various treatments with you, for example anti-depressants or sleeping pills.

Don't be pressurized into starting a course of medication if you feel that you can get through without chemical help. It is very easy to write a prescription but infinitely harder to kick a dependency to sleeping pills. However, if you are at the stage where you feel that you simply cannot cope without, then you must not be hard on yourself or feel that you have failed.

We estimate that at least half of our friends who have divorced have at some point had to resort to anti-depressants – and they served a very real purpose and got them through whilst they were at their lowest ebb. Just be aware that they can be difficult to come off in the long run and that, according to the particular brand you are prescribed, they can have serious side-effects. In the early weeks, for example, you may feel quite drowsy and even incapable of stringing a sentence together! If you need them, take them – however, if you need to have your wits about you, this can be a dangerous step to take. (See Chapter Five, 'Extreme Divorce'). If a brand is not working for you, do not be afraid to ask your GP for an alternative. It is your body and your health that is at stake and only you can decide what is right for you.

KNOWING WHO YOUR TRUE FRIENDS ARE

We all like to think that the majority of our friends will have our best interests at heart but, unfortunately, this is not always the case. It is important, therefore, to differ-entiate very early on between your real friends and your acquaintances. Some 'friends' will ask you intensely personal questions: 'what on earth made you marry him?' 'Surely the writing was on the wall when such and such happened?' 'Surely you must have seen her flirting with him?' 'Anyone with half a brain could have worked out that something was going on when he worked until midnight every night?' No matter how strong you are feeling, these kinds of comments can sting.

Prepare a stock answer for questions such as these and do *not* be pressurized into 'spilling your guts' or revealing intimate details. It is nobody's business except your own but your understandable desire to fathom what is happening to you by using friends as 'sounding boards' is likely to be misplaced in this instance. If your real friends are not available and you feel you must offload your emotions, write them down in a small notepad which you can carry with you in your handbag. This allows you to do *something* and then park the question. And it will make you feel instantly better. Then, when you get hold of your *real* friend, you can discuss it.

People do love to have something to gossip about and they positively relish being privy to 'special information' that they think you have told only them. They can then share it with everyone else and feel somehow important and superior to your other 'friends' (especially at the school gates and by the photocopier).

If your experience has been 'extreme', some will probably think that you are exaggerating or, even worse, barking mad and they are likely to communicate that fact to others. A woman whose children were at the same school as ours was heard to say loudly that we 'should knock heads together' and get back with our husband because she couldn't believe that our account could possibly be true as she had seen us at a social function months before looking perfectly 'OK'. And that was a member of the medical profession who should know rather better.

Both of us experienced the DPL (Dinner Party Lifecycle). This is the phenomenon where as a newly single female you are suddenly invited everywhere by your married friends/ acquaintances. You are exciting stuff. You are 'hot-off-the-press' in the popularity stakes and everyone wants you at their dinner parties so that they can grill you in company about your horror stories. Once your divorce is well underway, however, and you really are in need of the support of your friends, you are suddenly surplus to requirement. You are today's fish and chips paper and it can be intensely hurtful to realize that you had probably just been invited to be the evening's entertainment.

Post DPL you should also be aware that as an attractive woman you will metamorphose overnight from being party entertainment to being perceived as a threat by your married girlfriends. This is a very real phenomenon and you must expect that this will happen. The same does not ring true for men who continue to receive invitations post divorce since they are not a threat to the women – but could be regarded as an attractive appendage and female friends think they need a 'home-cooked meal'.

Divorce can be a lonely place for a woman, which is why it is *essential* to work out who your real friends are at the outset.

Real Friends Are Those Who:

- Make you feel good about yourself, support you and do not drain you.

- If your relationship has been acrimonious for some time or if you have been having a relationship with a bully or a womanizer, your self-esteem is likely to be at rock-bottom and you must be aware of this and make allowances for it. Make it a priority to see only those people who make you feel good about yourself and who will help you restore your self-confidence. No one has the right to put you down or make you feel inadequate. Other, perfectly well-meaning friends may unintentionally drain your energy because they are needy or demanding. Keep these friends at a distance, even if it is for a short time – certainly until you have re-charged your batteries and are feeling stronger.

- Are strong but kind.

- At times you will need a little bit of tough love. The truth may hurt from a real friend but they will be pointing out things that are in your best interests. And if you are smarting from the blow it may take a few days to get over, but believe us when we say that you are most likely to be better for the comment or observation.

- Say what they think to your face, not behind your back.

- It is very painful to learn that a 'friend' has betrayed you by talking negatively behind your back. If this should happen, never decide that it was a 'one-off' and that it won't happen again. A real friend will never gossip about you at all and will want to protect you from those who would like to put you down.

Here are a few tips that worked for us:

- Don't 'sweat the small stuff', as the Americans say.

- Don't worry about minutiae – you have enough on your plate.

- Continue to be there for your children and your close friends and family but leave the 'fair-weather' friends to fend for themselves. You know who they are – the ones who will take emotionally from you until you are suddenly in need of some support yourself – at which point you will find that they disappear in a cloud of dust.

- Become an 'occasional' ostrich. Emotional preparation is extremely important. We found that whilst a level of 'ostrich' behaviour – i.e., burying your head in the sand – is positively beneficial, completely refusing to accept the stark reality of your situation is most definitely not. For example, we found in the early days that it was sometimes too emotionally painful to open letters from our solicitor. A good solution was to ask a close friend or family member to open letters for us! That way, they can relay the letter's contents gently and quickly and this method dispenses with procrastination and the heart-lurching, sinking feeling that comes from opening something when you are on your own.

- Keep your Home Ship Shape. Nothing is more draining and disheartening in the midst of emotional upheaval than to be surrounded by mess or dirt. Even though it may be the very last thing on your mind and you may be physically worn out, if you can possibly find the time and the energy it really is worth the effort. If you can afford it then consider employing a cleaner as this reduces pressure on you. Keeping your home de-cluttered and clean will have an enormously beneficial effect on your emotional well-being and buying a bunch of even the most inexpensive flowers will lighten your mood considerably.

REASSESS YOUR SUPPORT NETWORK

At this point you need to think very hard about who is going to form part of your support network.

GP

We have already established that it is a good idea to visit your GP. You should aim to do this, even if you do not feel you need anti-depressants or sleeping pills. If you have a good GP they will support you. You may find that you have all manner of niggling ailments that are stress-related. Back problems and tension headaches are common when you are under stress and you may need to be referred to an osteopath, for example.

Employer/HR Department

This is a decision that needs to be thought through, depending on the type of relationship you have with your boss or with your HR department. It can be beneficial to let someone at your work know what you are going through if you trust them because there are bound to be times when you are feeling that you cannot cope and need to take time off – either to replenish your batteries or to see your solicitor/attend court. If, however, you do not sufficiently trust your boss or feel that he or she may use the knowledge as an excuse to demote you, or indeed dismiss you, then it is clearly not a good idea to give any indication of your situation at all.

Neighbours

If you have a good relationship with your neighbours, it is advisable to inform them that you are going through a divorce (especially if there has been domestic violence and you or your home are at risk from your ex-husband). People really do love to help and as a single woman/mother you will suddenly find yourself totally responsible for all the practical maintenance issues around the property. Of course, you may be thoroughly versed in wielding ratchets and hammers, but if not you will find that you will need to very quickly learn how to mend things around your house and to do small repairs. A friendly neighbour is particularly good to show you how to do this. Alternatively, you could sign up for a local practical maintenance course (this is another good way to ensure you get yourself out and about during your separation).

PHYSICAL PREPARATION

KEEPING YOURSELF HEALTHY

If ever there is a time to keep yourself healthy and in shape – then this is it. The impact of a divorce on your body is not to be underestimated – and it is likely that you will be either pumped up on adrenalin or struggling with your energy levels. Your body is already under a great deal of stress – and whether you like it or not, this impacts on all your organs, particularly your liver and your heart. Stress is a killer and can cause an enormous amount of damage to your body.

WHAT IS STRESS?

Stress is your body's physical response to events that make you feel upset or threatened. It is the 'fight or flight' reflex, which is actually your body's way of trying to protect you. Stress energizes you, focuses your mind immediately on the event in hand and even gives you extra physical strength in order to cope with a life-threatening situation. All the above qualities are great if you are bungee-jumping off the top of a cliff but devastating to your immune system if the threatening situation is prolonged for any length of time – and with no end in sight. You can either tense up and become overwhelmingly agitated or withdraw from the situation completely (friends, society) and the worst situation possible is to experience a combination of both, i.e., tensing and freezing at the same time. This is one of the ways in which you can damage your body irreparably – you are literally carrying the stress in your frame and unable to move. These are the physical effects of deep-fog territory – some people may even find that they are unable to peel themselves off the sofa, so great is their 'paralysis'. You may start to feel muscle aches and pains that left untreated can even result in literal physical paralysis. Think of the Hunchback of Notre Dame and you are well on the way to understanding how he got there.

Physical Effects of Stress

- Aches and pains
- Stomach problems, e.g., diarrhoea or constipation or both!
- Chest pains
- Frequent illnesses
- Reduced sex drive
- Nausea
- Irritable bowel syndrome

Emotional Effects of Stress

- Increased moodiness
- Irritability
- Depression
- A sense of despair
- Isolation

Cognitive Effects of Stress

- Constant worrying
- Having negative thoughts
- Memory problems
- Bad judgement
- Difficulty in concentrating or focusing on anything – deep, deep fog!

Behavioural Effects of Stress

- Drinking or smoking more
- Sleeping too much or too little
- Procrastination
- Nervous habits such as nail-biting

Stress can very easily take over your life. Over time, it can cause high blood pressure, and an increased risk of heart attack and stroke. The key is **control**. When the stress in your life is so excessive that you no longer feel in control – then it is essential that you take action. Nothing is more important than your health.

ALCOHOL

As we all know, a glass or eight of wine really can help to anaesthetize things, but this in anything but moderation is one of the very worst things you can do to yourself when you are going through a divorce. Alcohol has a very bad effect on the liver (which is already under a great deal of strain) so keep it to a minimum – and try to have a good few nights off alcohol every week.

DIET

Diet is enormously influential in affecting the way you feel and look. Although it is likely that what you eat is the very last thing on your mind when you are going through a divorce, it really is worth making an effort to eat at least one or two nutritious foods every day. This will not only make you feel better but it has the most enormously beneficial effect on your looks – which is really important to your sense of well-being. Try to get a sufficient quantity of **protein** in your diet – this will ensure that your skin, hair and nails get in tip-top condition as these are the first things that are likely to show the damaging effects of stress.

Here are our top ten suggestions for easy-snacking nutritious foods for skin and hair:

1. Avocadoes
2. Almonds
3. Berries (blueberries, strawberries, raspberries)
4. Oranges
5. Eggs
6. Salmon
7. Kiwi
8. Spinach
9. Tomatoes
10. Bananas

SLEEP

Never underestimate the value of a good night's sleep to your sense of well-being. And if you need to ask your GP for sleeping pills to establish a regular sleeping routine for a few weeks then this is a beneficial thing to consider and you should not feel ashamed of resorting to this. Just remember that you are unique and what you are going through is a unique situation. The pressures of divorce can be like having a new-born baby and sleep can be difficult to achieve.

MAKE TIME TO RELAX

It really is important to 'switch off', even if it is just watching your favourite comedy series or soap. Do not feel that every waking moment should be used to progress your situation or to achieve a result, as this will dramatically increase your sense of pressure and will make it impossible for you to relax. Mindless distraction can be very beneficial! Any of the following can renew your sense of self and your sense

of well-being: acupuncture, massage, Pilates/Yoga, reading,
meditation, golf club/book club, swimming, walking the dog
or just socializing.

CHAPTER TWO

Preparing Your Child
for Separation

'To lose one parent may be regarded as a misfortune, to lose both looks careless.'

Oscar Wilde

THE REALITY OF PREPARING YOUR CHILD

Preparing your child for the fact that you are on the verge of separating is crucial and, understandably, you are likely to feel that it is one of the most difficult things that you will ever have to do. Separation turns a child's world upside down and that is why it is imperative to get the transition right.

Recent statistics (2012) demonstrate that a staggering 64 per cent of children affected by divorce are under the age of eleven and that 21 per cent are under the age of five. However, many more children experience parental separation each year that are not included in such statistics because their parents were never married. No matter what the exact numbers, it is certain that there are many tens of thousands of very young children who are affected by separation every year. Again, it is worth remembering that you are not alone!

It is likely that you will have all sorts of preconceived ideas about what you should and should not say to your children and about the way that they will react. You are also likely to have a stock of fears about how such things are likely to affect children garnered from films, books and the 'pseudo' psychology that is everywhere in our navel-gazing society. For example, most of us will have heard that a person's view of life and any subsequent emotional problems will have their root in memories and traumatic experiences that happened during childhood. The good news is that if the process is handled with sufficient sensitivity and preparation, then the majority of children will not suffer any long-term effects (Children's Society website).

It is hardly surprising that breaking up a home and creating a new one is going to have an enormous impact on a child – and their reaction is going to have an enormous impact on *you*. It is also disturbing to think that the 'fallout' of separation and divorce may not be seen in a child for many years. The treatment rooms of psychiatrists and counsellors alike are constantly replenished by young adults who are coming to terms with the loss of their family unit many years after the event. Therefore, it is worth being very aware of, and alert to, your child's reactions during the process if you can because these can give you an indication of how they are going to cope with the process down the line. For example, if a child bottles up his emotions now, the chances are that they are going to come out amplified at a much later date. In this instance it might be worth enlisting professional help to try to see whether your child can start working through their emotions before they get too overwhelming.

Whatever the reason behind the decision to separate, a child can feel as though his/her whole world has fallen apart and the intensity of their upset can be devastating to watch. As their mother you are biologically programmed to want to care for and nurture your child. It is in your DNA.

THE MALE BRAIN

Your child's father also has natural behaviours embedded in his DNA – men are equally programmed at a biological level to protect and ensure that their offspring are physically safe. Unfortunately, this is sometimes implemented in such a 'male brain' way that we women inevitably feel threatened and even frightened by the father's behaviour during separation. It is the different way in which males and females are hard-wired to 'protect' their offspring that can cause so much of the acrimony in divorce. Some women protect their offspring by shrouding and enveloping them to such an extent that fathers perceive – sometimes rightly – a barrier forming that will separate them from their children. (There is no doubt that many a divorcing woman would prefer that her ex just didn't exist.) It is that feeling of exclusion that is at the heart of many contact disputes. As a man they then try to break through that barrier (often aggressively), which in turn can frighten the mothers – who then react in turn by 'protecting' their offspring further – and so a vicious circle forms. A common tactic is the 'tit for tat' residence application – 'I can't see the children so I'll take them off her and see how she likes it'. Avoid this situation at all costs – it will make you and your children's lives miserable.

Our advice is to try to put aside your feelings of fear, if you can, and look at the facts and your children's behaviour. Unless there is actual evidence of abusive behaviour towards the children – the most obvious being that the children just do not want to spend time alone with their father – make sure that you fully share the children with him. Let him know what they are up to, make sure he has copies of school photos and reports, knows about parents' evenings, let him see where they live and sleep when with you and, most importantly of all, allow him extensive and ideally flexible contact if it is feasible. This may all seem counter intuitive but it is likely that, once his male brain realizes that his offspring are 'protected and safe' in their new home with you and that he is not being excluded, he will be less aggressive about contact, particularly if he is distracted by the attentions of another woman in his life. Such an approach requires real strength on your behalf and may prove to be difficult without support, but if you can achieve it, it will almost certainly save you and the children a huge amount of bitter upset and wrangling. What's more, it is likely to succeed in attaining at least the same, if not a better, long-term outcome, at significantly lower cost, than arguing over contact through lawyers and the courts.

THE EMOTIONAL FALLOUT

It is almost inevitable that you will experience a degree of guilt in the early months, no matter what the rights and wrongs of the separation. In our view it is never the right thing to stay together for the sake of the children and we all know people who shy away from marriage because of the atrocious relationship of their parents who stayed together for their sake. A woman in her early twenties who we shall call Sarah explains: 'I remember in my early teens the absolute terror when my mother called up the stairs that Sunday lunch was ready. It was the only meal we ever sat down to eat together. Thank goodness for that. My parents stuck together for me and my brothers and sisters. It was so obvious to me aged fourteen that my parents barely liked each other, let alone loved each other and subsequently Sunday lunches were dreadful and dreaded.' As Sarah grew up, she took every opportunity to avoid being at home with her parents who bickered constantly – and if they were not at each other's throats there was an awkward, tension-loaded silence. When her parents finally split in her late teens, she found that she could actually have a relationship with her parents separately and she mourned those wasted years.

Obviously, the degree of upset that children feel can vary according to the way in which the break-up is handled, but the age of the child, their level of understanding and the support that they receive from both parents, the whole family and their friends will be a good indication as to what you can expect.

A child may feel an enormous sense of **loss** – especially if they are losing their home or having to change school all in one heart-wrenching go. They may be catapulted into a completely new and unfamiliar environment – for example, if one of the parents has created a new relationship and the new partner has dependent children. They can be extremely **angry** at one or both of their parents for causing the separation, at the same time as feeling **guilty** that they were the cause of the break-up. They will almost certainly feel **insecure** and even emotionally torn because they feel a sense of divided loyalty. They may even fear abandonment on the basis that if one parent can go then perhaps the other is capable of doing the same.

Whatever the dynamics, it is extremely likely that divorce will add financial strain to an already difficult situation and this can be devastating for a child – especially if they have to be taken out of school and away from their friends or have to move to another part of town when they are already at their most vulnerable.

GIVING EMOTIONAL SUPPORT TO YOUR CHILD

THINGS YOU CAN DO TO HELP YOUR CHILD:

- Talk to your child as much as you can – and be open. Give them the opportunity to ask questions and never appear to be too busy to communicate with them. Emotions do not run to a timetable and their feelings must be heard and acknowledged the moment they arise – even it if means postponing a commitment to someone else.

- Make sure that your child knows that they still have two parents who love them and who will continue to love them – no matter what.

- Try to protect your child from grown-up concerns and responsibilities and under no circumstances try to turn them into *your* supporters (which is a understandable thing to want to do) – they have enough to deal with without worrying about how *you* are coping with the process. Maintaining a strong façade is tough, especially if you are hurting or very angry yourself, but it really is vital in affording your child a real sense of security. We are not saying that you should never show emotion – it is essential that you are always *authentic* for your children. It is just better to do the majority of your grieving when they are not around.

- Keep the routine going! Aim to continue doing as much of your family's normal activities as possible and keep seeing lots of friends and family and doing fun things together. This will make your child feel as though life is relatively normal. It doesn't need to be expensive. It could be something as simple as curling up together on the sofa with a DVD and a bowl of popcorn.

- Ensure your child knows that the separation is the parents' fault and has nothing to do with anything that your child has done. They will always think it is their fault – it is imperative that you tell them frequently so that they really understand. You may think you have told them but you must say it every day.

- Find the time to be with your child. Prioritize them in your diary and in your life – you will never regret it!

- Always be reliable. We have all experienced occasions when we have promised a child something in good faith only for something unforeseen to intervene – like a crisis that keeps you at work, for example. When it comes to making plans – particularly for parental contact – it is critical that you are seen to be dependable so that they can retain a sense of stability and security. Never make a promise that you cannot keep. If you are not one hundred per cent certain that you can do something it is better to say that you are unable to make a promise than to let them down. That way they will always trust you and realize that you are reliable.

- Always make your child feel that you are interested in their views but at the same time make it perfectly clear that you are the adult who makes the decisions. It is very easy to give your child so much say in what happens – in a misguided effort to make them feel integral to the life of the family – that they end up getting hurt and disappointed. A good example of this is taking your children to house viewings post-divorce. They will be seeing a property from a child's viewpoint and this is unlikely to encompass practicalities such as the size of a mortgage, access to public transport and the level of council tax! Make your decision and then tell them.

- Always try to encourage a healthy and loving bond between your children and their father and never forget that a child's love for a parent is unconditional. The exception to this is where there has been an abusive relationship or some other exceptional reason (see Chapter Five, 'Extreme Divorce').

- Help them to prepare stock answers so that when they are asked at school where their father is, they are armed with sufficiently strong answers. Test them on this – encourage them to be strong. Bullies love to pick on vulnerable children and a divorce can make your child a prime target for bullies. Some examples might be:

- Q: Why did your parents split up?
- A: Because they didn't get on any more.

- Q: Does your mum have a boyfriend?
- A: You may not, for obvious reasons, have shared the existence of a new man in your life with your children. So the best answer would be 'no' because a 'yes' has follow-on questions like: Is he your new dad? Does he live with you? This answer helps to simplify your child's life.

- Q: Do you see your dad?
- A: Yes – unless the answer is 'no'. But 'yes' means that you have to have the follow-on conversations – like when? So the stock answer is: 'Yes – on weekends.'

THINGS TO AVOID DOING:

- Don't involve your children in the minutiae of the separation at all if you can avoid it. Don't talk about going to court or of receiving horrid papers in the post. Tell your real friends instead (see Chapter One, 'Preparing to Divorce').

• Don't criticize your ex or try to undermine him in front of your child – they will resent you for it no matter how good your intention or your desire to get them to understand the reality. Even if your ex is a bully, he is still their father. If your ex has done something to let them (or you) down say he is being 'silly' or 'busy'. Use a child's vocabulary – it will help to defuse the fear.

• Never ask your child to take sides. This can be something as seemingly harmless as asking them where they would like to spend Christmas or whether they prefer spending the holidays with Grandma Phoebe or Grandpa Percy.

• Never use your child as a 'weapon' to try to hurt or get back at your ex, no matter how strong the temptation or how justifiable it might seem to you. They will feel manipulated and it will make them feel even more isolated and alone than before.

• Don't give the impression that a child must step into the shoes of your ex in any capacity whatsoever or ask them to shoulder any kind of adult responsibility.

• Be careful about introducing newcomers to your home, particularly if you have started a new relationship. Have strong rules about when and how they are positioned in your life – especially about the issue of overnight or weekend stays. Children can easily feel displaced and threatened by a new man in their home. It is important to remember that they will continue to feel like this – even into adulthood.

- Keep public displays of affection in a new relationship to a minimum or preferably to none at all. This ensures that you do not unwittingly rub your child's nose in your new relationship.

THE CHILD BRAIN

The age of your child will be a very important indicator as to what reaction you can expect and therefore how best to communicate the news – although character and gender also play an enormous part in how you should consider handling the situation.

Younger Children

As a general rule it seems sensible that the younger the child, the less information you should give them. There is no need to put the fear of God into them by talking about moving house if it is something that is not likely to happen for a couple of years. It is important to remember that time is very different to young children. They will not know when 'Saturday' is – or how long a weekend stay lasts.

The exception to this is where repetition is necessary. Here is an example of a seven-year-old's view of going to boarding school: his parents dropped him off on his first day of term with his trunk, tuck-box, and new school uniform. He later confessed to his mother that he had been devastated to discover that he was expected to stay at the school and was not returning home with his sister and parents. His mother could not believe that the concept had not filtered through to him after so many conversations – and the packing up of his duvet, pyjamas, etc. It is worthwhile remembering that it is important to reinforce any message that you feel necessary – ad nauseam, i.e., 'You will be at Daddy's for two sleeps…'

Older Children/Teenagers

Older children may manifest their upset by misbehaving or withdrawing. They may find it difficult to concentrate at school, which is doubly hard if they are in the process of swotting for exams. They are also likely to ask a lot of questions – and these will inevitably include questions that you find upsetting or embarrassing. Why don't you get on any more? Does Daddy have a girlfriend? Is it because of me? It is understandable that you might want to derail or block such questions but it is vital to answer these questions as honestly and as fully as possible to avoid the inevitable misinterpretation of events. Be prepared that even though you may have separated when they were very young, at some point they will ask the same questions as older children would do. This can really unsettle you because you probably felt that they had come to terms with the living arrangements and the family structure, etc.

Girls

Girls have a very different psychology from boys – they need to talk things through again and again and they process their feelings by saying what they feel out loud. Give them as much opportunity as possible to 'offload' their feelings, to talk and grieve out loud. They will probably want to ask you the same questions again and again and you must try to be patient with this – it is a very important step towards acceptance and moving on with their lives.

Boys

Boys are psychologically predisposed to come to terms with things more quickly than girls. They weigh up the options in their minds very quickly and are more likely to make decisions before girls.

The 'Only' Child

Only children are different. They do not have siblings who can support them and divorce can hit them particularly hard. It is important to make allowances for this and to ensure that they see their friends as often as possible.

OTHER POINTS TO CONSIDER:

- Safety

  The safety and security of your children is of paramount importance and you should take extra steps to put fool-proof procedures and drills in place when you are going through a separation, especially if contact is in dispute or your ex is not allowed to see them (see Chapter Five, 'Extreme Divorce').

- Mobile Phones

  Although mobile phones are clearly an additional expense at a time when you do not need any – it is advisable to ensure that your child has a mobile phone that they can carry around with them at all times not only for emergencies, but for the times when they feel that they need to call you if they are feeling upset or confused. Clearly mobile phones should be age appropriate. Many providers will give you a free phone with a contract or pay-as you-go is a good option as long as you remember to check the amount of minutes on the phone regularly so that your child is always able to call you.

- Telephone directory of essential contacts

  Make sure that your child has a list of numbers of key people should they need to call: carers, grandparents, godparents, neighbours and friends.

- **Police/Fire/Ambulance**
  It is an obvious one but make sure that your child knows to
  ring 999 in an emergency. Put a list on the fridge, including
  emergency numbers. Make sure they know the UK number
  and do not automatically quote '911' from watching too much
  American TV!

- **Fire Drill**
  Make sure that you have a fire drill in your home so that should
  a fire break out in your house, even in the middle of the night,
  they will know exactly what to do and where to go.

- **Code Word**
  Have a code that only you and your children know so that it can
  be used even in public. This is especially useful in awkward or
  embarrassing situations and it will alert you and your children
  to the fact that you need to leave urgently. Your code can be an
  entire sentence like 'I think you left the oven on' or something
  equally innocuous – anything so long as it works for you.

WHO SHOULD YOU INFORM?

Schools

It is important to inform your child's school about what
is happening – not least because you will want them to let
you know whether they see any changes in the behaviour or
academic progress of your child. Give them your ex's new
address and contact details too and ask them to copy him
about parents' evenings, school reports and photos, etc. This
prevents the ex from feeling excluded, which in turn prevents confrontation. It is also essential to provide them with
copies of any court Child Arrangement Orders (previously

known as contact or residence orders or prohibited steps orders) or non-molestation injunctions, etc., so that they can take the appropriate steps regarding your child's security at the school. Do not be embarrassed or ashamed about your family circumstances. They have seen it all before and will be grateful that you have taken the time to let them know what is happening. Doing this also ensures that the school can take every possible security precaution which will add to your peace of mind.

Doctor

It is always a good idea to inform your GP about the separation if you take your child to see him. For example, if your child has suddenly started to wet the bed or to have stomach pains it is likely that this will be a psychosomatic symptom of their emotional upset and your GP will need to take this into consideration when making a diagnosis.

Grandparents

If your separation is an acrimonious one it is more than likely that your ex's family will take his side and it is quite possible that communication will have broken down between you and them. Although you may feel quite justified in severing ties with his parents, never forget that they are your child's grandparents and you should try to ensure that your child continues to have a relationship with them if this is at all possible. The exception to this is if there has been an abusive relationship, in which case this scenario is clearly impossible. If this is too difficult then perhaps work with your lawyer to set up a way of them having contact through a facilitator or friend or intermediary if this makes you and the children feel more comfortable.

COMMON SENSE V THE LAW

Where?

Be aware when you are considering filing for divorce that it is crucial to know *where* to do it. In some countries, children become wards of court the moment you file for divorce. This would put you in the unenviable and nightmarish position of not being able to take your children out of the country until the divorce is final.

Locks

Solicitors will tell you that you are not legally entitled to change the locks should your ex have moved out. This is generally true but common sense is key here. Your ex is hardly going to take you to court over it (see Chapter Five, 'Extreme Divorce') nor is any judge likely to order you to hand over a key if there is a real question over your security or any threat to you or your children. If you have to do this, write to your ex explaining why you have done it (keeping a copy, as always), what you are afraid might happen and make it clear that you are quite prepared to allow him into the property at an agreed time in the presence of a third party, e.g., a parent or friend (you may well not even be there) for him to remove agreed possessions, etc. This leaves him with very little to complain about.

Stick To Your Guns

Don't be pressurized by lawyers if you think your choices for your children are correct. No one knows your children as well as you do. But do *listen* to them, even if they are saying what you don't want to hear: they are likely to have a better grasp of how the courts will approach matters than you do. Remember they are on your side.

Children need the security of a routine, particularly if their world is falling about their ears. In order to work, contact arrangements need to be: Consistent. Predictable. Reliable.

EMOTIONAL AND BEHAVIOURAL PROBLEMS

Emotional and behavioural problems in children are significantly more common when their parents are separating. The insecurity that the child feels can mean that they start to behave as if they are much younger than before. **Bedwetting, nightmares, clinginess, misbehaving or withdrawing** are all ways that children can demonstrate their inner turmoil and it is interesting that such behaviour often happens immediately before or immediately after contact with a parent from whom they have been separated.

EATING DISORDERS

Eating disorders are an obvious (if not an immediately visible) reaction for a child going through the emotional turmoil of a family break-up. According to the Office for National Statistics, one in ten children aged between five and sixteen has a mental health disorder and about 1 per cent of those has an eating disorder. Eating disorders tend to manifest themselves in the teenage years, peaking around the age of sixteen. Interestingly, almost 50 per cent of people with eating disorders also meet the criteria for depression (ANAD – National Association of Anorexia Nervosa and Associated Disorders USA).

Anorexia Nervosa

This eating disorder is based on a distorted body image and the sufferer will have an irrational fear of getting fat. He or she will greatly reduce the amount of food they consume or even starve themselves completely in order to reduce their bodily fat deposits. The average number of calories consumed by an anorexic is 600 to 800 per day. This disorder has nothing to do with looking good or healthy and there is usually an element of control involved. This is particularly true in a divorce situation where a child can feel 'out of control' and as if the only way they can wield an element of control over their lives is by restricting what they put into their bodies.

The good news is that, according to the US National Comorbidity Replication Study, the average duration of anorexia is 1.7 years, and between 80 and 95 per cent will recover completely. Relapse is common, however, especially in the first year after recovery.

Bulimia Nervosa

This eating disorder is a cycle of bingeing on food and then purging through vomiting or taking laxatives or diuretics. This is not as common as anorexia – nor is it as easy to spot, for the simple reason that the body weight does not change. Bulimia can produce serious long-term effects – not least from the complications of rotten teeth from frequent vomiting.

SELF-HARMING

Self-harming is characterized by making cuts in, scratching or burning of the skin and even swallowing sharp objects. A staggering one in fifteen young people have confessed to self-harming at some point and additional evidence suggests that the UK rates of self-harm are higher than anywhere in the rest of Europe (Wikipedia).

Finally, it is important to remember that even though the process of separation is traumatic and hugely disruptive, it can still be a gift. Your children can gain incredible insights into human nature by the experience of watching their parents' relationship. It can make them very perceptive, very awake human beings and if you support them sufficiently through the process there are many things that they will learn about relationships from which they will benefit their whole lives. Single mothers have the opportunity to make their children strong and great achievers. You will have had to fight so hard to keep the status quo in the beginning that your over-compensation is likely to have produced enormous benefits in your children. Your 'survivor' attitude will make them strong and they are likely to find the normal hurdles that life throws at them along the way easier than others might. They may even achieve more as a result.

If you are finding it difficult to help your child adjust, you may want to seek outside help and advice. Your GP will be able to offer support and advice, but in more extreme circumstances the local **child and adolescent mental health service** is a good place to start.

USEFUL ORGANIZATIONS

- Action for Children – Supports families through divorce, bereavement and children's behavioural problems. www.actionforchildren.org.uk

- Citizens Advice Bureau – Your local branch is listed in the telephone directory. www.citizensadvice.org.uk

- Counselling Directory www.counselling-directory.org.uk

- Divorce Aid is run by an independent group of professionals and provides advice, support and information on all aspects of divorce. It has specialized sections for both young children and teenagers, which empowers them to recognize and deal with emotions that arise from separation and divorce. www.divorceaid.co.uk

- Family Lives (Parentline Plus) offers help and advice to parents on bringing up children and teenagers. www.familylives.org.uk

- National Family Mediation is an organization specifically set up to help families who are separating. It has a useful booklist, which includes books for children of different ages. www.nfm.org.uk

- Relate – Helps couples with relationship difficulties. www.relate.org.uk

- The Children's Society – Produces a series of leaflets for children and parents and a useful and informative website. www.childrenssociety.org.uk

- The Money Advice Service – Information and advice on the financial aspects of divorce, separation or civil partnership dissolution, including an interactive calculator to help you manage finances, work out what you have and what you owe, and help you to consider how you might split what you have between you. www.moneyadviceservice.org.uk

CHAPTER THREE

How to File for Divorce

*'Get action. Seize the moment. Man was never intended to become
an oyster...'*

Theodore Roosevelt

And so the time has finally arrived. You have made the monumental decision to separate – and now is the time to begin legal proceedings and file for divorce.

CHOOSING A SOLICITOR

The very first thing you will need to do is to choose a solicitor. Of course, you may be proposing to represent yourself, but such a decision should be taken with extreme caution. If you are dealing with complex financial, child contact and maintenance issues then to appoint a solicitor is virtually a prerequisite – and you must prepare yourself for this eventuality.

Health Warning: Be aware that should you decide to represent yourself through the courts as a '**litigant in person**' there are many pitfalls to trip you up. You may think that it is a way to save yourself vast sums of money, but not only is it deeply stressful to represent yourself, you simply cannot compete in a dispute with another law firm (that your ex has probably appointed) unless you have a good knowledge of the relevant laws and the way that the courts work. Represent yourself at your peril! If you do decide that there is no alternative for you then The Personal Support Unit – www.thepsu.org – offers emotional and practical advice to individuals representing themselves, **however**, *they do not provide any form of legal advice.*

Choosing a solicitor can be done in a number of ways and personal recommendation is arguably the best. However, it is important to be aware that a solicitor that has successfully worked for someone else just might not work for you. Chemistry is vital when selecting the advisor with whom you will be working on such an intimate level.

Another route is by referral through a firm that you have already instructed on another matter. The final route is the Internet. As with all Internet searches, you will be bombarded by a dazzling array of firms all purporting to give unparalleled advice at unmatchable prices. It is a daunting prospect to phone up a solicitor and say, 'I want to file for divorce, can you help me?' Brace yourself, and make that call.

ACT SMART

It is also easy to think that the most expensive solicitor is the best. This is simply not the case. Sometimes the priciest lawyers can be the most cut-throat and the most inflexible – and some of these will be more concerned with lining their own wallets than with helping you to get the best and cheapest outcome. Be astute and trust your instinct.

It is common practice that legal firms will give you one hour of advice for free – and it is important to check this before arranging an appointment. Clearly this is to position themselves and their credentials as customary and fair. However, in the course of the meeting they will typically advise you only on 'the generic process' and not on your specific case. You will need your passport, utility bills and other documents, which they will ask for prior to the meeting in the event that you do decide to instruct them and this acts as a platform against which they will ask for a deposit. This will be held and used in the first instance as your down payment to engage their services to represent you. If you do this and then do not instruct them, they will return the deposit to you.

In many cases people use a local firm of solicitors (having done little research) in order to speed up the process. It is important to note that you will be charged in this instance and the deposit will be used as a fee for processing your application. This firm will then pass your file onto the firm you decide will ultimately progress your case.

IMPORTANT POINTS TO CONSIDER:

- When handing over the case you will need a further deposit and will need to spend more time briefing your new solicitor. This will typically be an hour of the solicitor's time. In the event that your solicitor leaves the firm or changes role during the proceedings, be aware that you will be approached to pay for the new solicitor to be briefed.

- Always challenge additional fees. You engaged the firm for its services and in many cases you will have been given no choice in the solicitor you were given – it is their duty of care to hand over the case in a diligent fashion to another solicitor at the firm. Do not accept the fees associated with handovers and firmly point out that it was the firm's decision to alter the details of your contract with them. (For further information visit: www.lawsociety.org.uk)

SOME THINGS TO BEAR IN MIND

Once you have made the sensible decision to appoint a solicitor, there are a couple of fundamental things to bear in mind: you will need to work extremely closely with your solicitor during the course of the divorce proceedings and you may have to share some intimate and even unsavoury details about your marriage with him or her.

The term 'working with' your solicitor is key here. You are the client and it is easy to forget this for the simple reason that your solicitor will be handling the most personal aspects of your life and those most dear to you, if you have children. You are paying for their services – we will address later in this chapter how you can keep your costs to a tightly managed minimum – but some costs and fees are inevitable and unavoidable when you choose to go down the legal route, and you should be aware of this.

It is really important to note that whilst solicitors can advise and present you with the legal options, it is not for them to tell you what to do. Whatever steps you choose to take are completely and ultimately your own decision. This applies to anything that you do at any stage of the divorce. You make the decisions and at times this can feel deeply frustrating.

You will almost certainly be paying your solicitor by the hour and it is hardly surprising that you might feel justified in wanting them to take the decisions for you in order to take some of the burden off your shoulders. Some of this desire will be to do with the 'deep fog' state that we referred to earlier. Your world is an unstable one and you understandably long for someone to 'take charge' and tell you what to do. This is just not going to happen and you must prepare yourself for this.

You will not be given a 'Service Level Agreement' by

your solicitor (in the same way that your sink will be unblocked by your plumber or your clutch fixed at your garage). And further down the line you will be at the mercy of the court system and the judge – and the mood of all concerned. You will feel like screaming at times with the inevitable delays and frustrated by the lengths you will have to go to. Just remember that it is a process and if you **work smart** and really engage with your solicitor you can circumvent some of the problems and obstacles that you will encounter along the way.

So whilst this might seem a travesty of justice, it is just the way things are. But in our cases, and in the cases of so many others, had it not been for solicitors and the legal system we would simply not have achieved a successful outcome. You cannot do it on your own.

Another essential point to remember is that that you can say **stop** at any stage in the proceedings if you wish to reconcile or even just pause if the situation is becoming too intense to bear. You can. It is your decision – at all times.

It is quite possible that this may be the first time you have come into real contact with the legal profession. It can be quite daunting – even intimidating – and alongside all the other areas of your life you are now managing on your own, it will come as no surprise that this aspect of the divorce proceedings will take up a considerable amount of your time. It can be a full-time job getting divorced! It will also require some 'good-quality' thinking time.

You will be confronted with legal terms and jargon at every turn and we have provided in this book simple explanations of the basic terms and references to help you. It is very easy to sit opposite your lawyer in a meeting and nod sagely because you genuinely believe you fully understand the point of law being explained or discussed. However, by the time you have got on the train or driven to pick the children up from school or put in another shift at work, you might find that your understanding has been diluted or even completely forgotten. The exact terms or nuance relating to your specific situation will have been lost. Our advice is to have a notebook to hand and to **take copious notes** that you can refer to later.

Never be afraid to ask for things to be repeated and if you don't understand just say so – and ask questions there and then. Don't worry about appearing stupid or ignorant. Asking questions is essential to really understanding the process, especially since all the pressure you are under is going to make it exceedingly difficult for you to concentrate. Your solicitor will understand this if you have chosen them wisely. You are paying for the call or the meeting so make sure you get the outcomes and answers you need **at the time** so that you are in a position to make the necessary decisions. If not, you will only have to call your lawyer or send an email the next day and you will effectively be charged twice for the same piece of information. There are a number of ways to approach the proceedings and on your first meeting with a solicitor you will be asked to think about other less adversarial options such as mediation.

We are going to highlight the key stages of the process and whilst we cannot cover every twist and turn and eventuality, we will offer some guidance as to how to navigate through the key phases.

LEGAL AID

Legal Aid has taken on 'mythological' proportions in the imagination of the nation and everywhere we go we hear from people who think that Legal Aid is a 'fall-back' solution should things go wrong for them. This could not be further from the truth.

From April 2013, Legal Aid is no longer available to the vast majority of families who are divorcing. Prior to this, people on low incomes were considered eligible to apply for Legal Aid (paid for by the Government) and all matters relating to divorce were covered – e.g., financial settlements, contact and residence disputes over children and domestic abuse.

Under the new rules, Legal Aid is limited to those who can *prove* that: they have been a victim of domestic violence (psychological, physical, sexual, financial or emotional – and this now includes where there has been controlling behaviour, e.g., preventing access to moneys or verbal abuse); they have a child who is at risk of abduction outside the UK, or they are under threat of forced marriage.

Only those who are receiving income support of any kind such as Jobseekers' Allowance are still eligible for Legal Aid. If you are not receiving benefits, you must be able to prove that your income and your assets are within their current financial limits. Visit: www.gov.uk/check-legal-aid for a Legal Aid checker and eligibility.

These changes have resulted in a massive reduction in the number of cases receiving Legal Aid each year. According to Citizens Advice, only 40,000 cases will be eligible each year compared with a historic figure of some 250,000.

It is important to note that if you are co-habiting with

someone, even if he is not your husband, his income and assets will also be taken into account.

In any event, the statutory charges (although much lower than a typical solicitor's hourly rate) are required to be repaid.

DIRECT OR PUBLIC ACCESS

It is no longer a requirement to instruct a solicitor before a barrister can work for you and nowadays you can appoint a barrister to represent you directly. Many barristers now do direct-access work and they offer reduced fees for those on low incomes. An added advantage of this approach is that it allows the individual client to ask for legal help only when it is required so it is cost-effective and bills do not mount up unnecessarily.

MEDIATION

The UK Government has, for many years, attempted to provide a more conciliatory approach to separation and divorce by steering people into mediation in order to resolve issues and areas of conflict (Family Law Act 1999) and it is now **mandatory** in almost all disputes concerning children.

You will have a good idea by now whether you think mediation will work for you and your husband. In general, mediation works when both parties genuinely want to reach a deal. It is a process of assisted negotiation through an independent third party who acts as a sort of honest broker between the two sides. If you believe that you and he are both capable of rationally discussing the aspects of your separation, child contact and division of assets without descending into a heated and emotional argument, then this needs to be explored on the advice of your solicitors.

Mediators can cost roughly the same as a solicitor (for the good ones) and therefore you must be conscious and astute about your own situation and consider whether this is a sensible way to spend your joint money and your time. If mediation breaks down, then you are back to the drawing board and to the court process. For mediation costs refer to the Family Mediation Association website at: www.thefma.co.uk/family/mediation. These can be on an hourly, sessional or case basis. Alternatively visit: www. justice.gov.uk/courts/mediation.

COLLABORATIVE DIVORCE

The collaborative law process is promoted (along with other non-court processes such as mediation and arbitration) by the Resolution organization. Resolution includes some 6,500 family lawyers and other professionals as members, all of whom are committed to following a non-confrontational code of practice.

Each side appoints their own collaboratively trained lawyer, and they then all meet in a series of 'four-way' face-to-face meetings in order to try to work things out. Both of you will have your lawyer by your side throughout the process to offer support and legal advice.

You and your lawyers then sign an agreement that commits you to trying to resolve the issues without going to court and **prevents them from representing you in court** if the collaborative process breaks down.

Collaborative Lawyers can be found at: www.resolution. org.uk.

SEPARATION

Once you and your husband decide to separate, you won't be living together any more, but nor will you be divorced. A legal separation agreement is essential if you've decided to separate permanently as an alternative to divorce. In order to adequately protect yourself, you will need everything to be rubber-stamped by the court so that if either of you fails to keep to your part of the agreement, the other party can ask the court to enforce it.

Other instances when a legal separation agreement is essential include times when:

- You're separating as a precursor to divorce
- You're so estranged from your husband that communication and cooperation are unworkable
- You simply don't trust your husband to keep his promises
- One of you wants spousal support
- Minors are involved (under 18)

LEGAL SEPARATION

Whilst a 'Do it Yourself' approach is possible, the agreement will need to be rubber-stamped by a solicitor or a court.

Health Warning: couples can go down the route of a legal separation for all manner of reasons. Perhaps it seems less final and appears to be financially beneficial as an interim step or as a more rapid, less aggressive approach to ending the relationship. It can also be used by one party as prevarication in the hope of 'spinning things out'.

FULL-FAT DIVORCE

However, if either of you decide at a later date that you wish to divorce 'for real' because you have a new partner in your life, one or both parties fails to adhere to their obligations or the legal agreement has not lived up to its original spirit, you will be in the unenviable position of having to renegotiate the terms of a 'full-fat' divorce. This can make you feel as though you are separating all over again and can resurrect painful emotions and grudges. Make sure that you appraise yourself of all the contingencies of setting up a legal separation agreement and the term you anticipate it to be in place for (and be realistic here) and whether or not it is robust enough to stand the test of time. Don't sign anything that you do not fully understand and ensure you cover all aspects.

MANAGING YOUR SOLICITOR'S TIME AND YOUR MONEY

This is the difficult bit – and the bit where you will need to be extremely disciplined. It is entirely understandable that you will want to offload your feelings and frustrations about your soon-to-be-ex-husband. However, your solicitor is not a counsellor – you would need to pay for that separately! He or she is there to provide legal advice – not emotional support – and it is very easy to forget this. Therefore, when going to a meeting or having a call with your solicitor, work out your objectives in advance: what do you want to achieve (and be realistic about this)? How long will you need to do this, e.g., fifteen minutes or an hour? Always note the time at which you start the call and the time you finish. And remember that the pleasantries cost money – a nice hello and 'how are you?' is fine; 'how were the holidays and what did you do at Christmas?', etc., is a costly courtesy. This does not mean you need to avoid building a relationship with your solicitor. That is vital and you do need to have an open and transparent relationship in order to be able to decide on your course of action.

Skype and conference calls are useful second-best options for meetings further down the line. Do try to keep the meetings face-to-face post your initial meetings if you possibly can as you then have the opportunity to ask a lot of questions and really understand the situation, which isn't always easy on the telephone. The initial briefing meeting typically lasts an hour to an hour and a half and once you have appointed your solicitor there may be one or two further preparation and exploratory meetings. These should last approximately two to three hours in total. These briefing meetings will be to go through your situation in fine detail and you will then be asked to prepare some documentation – such as a financial breakdown for the household in relation to maintenance for your children and yourself.

For your initial briefing, break your 'story' down into three key areas:

- Children
- Financial matters (assets, maintenance)
- The general state of the relationship between you and your husband

Prior to any meeting or call, make a plan:

- Objectives – what is the purpose of the call? List the questions you want to ask
- Outcomes – what do you want to achieve?
- Timelines – what are the next steps in the process or phase? It is always good to ask this in every meeting to re-confirm the pace of the process

During any meeting or call, write down your solicitor's responses. Get everything down as you understand it there and then and repeat it back to your solicitor to ensure you have fully understood. If as a result of your discussions you are required to make a decision, take your time. If necessary take it away and go back to your solicitor with a succinct email of instruction.

It will be tough to share some of the intimate aspects of your marriage. The legal process is at best relentless and at worst exasperating. Practise articulating things to your solicitor out loud – especially if you are in a highly charged emotional climate with your husband. By rehearsing, you can take the intense personal emotion out of what you need to say and you can also hear how your words will come across. This does not mean that you should underplay how you are feeling or how the divorce is impacting on you, but it will give your solicitor the best chance to support you. You need to be prepared and focused.

Letters, emails, orders and applications/pleadings must be read by you thoroughly – perhaps several times. Ensure you fully understand the language and the implications. Legal language is not always that simple. If you have a trusted friend or family member it is sometimes good to ask their opinion. However, nothing replaces the advice of your solicitor so bear that in mind. They are acting for you and they do have your family's best interests at heart.

CONTEMPORANEOUS NOTES

These can be a nightmare but you will thank yourself for keeping a really good record of conversations, texts and experiences. In the throes of divorce it is vital to keep this as an aide-memoire of things, dates and events to furnish your applications or discussions with your solicitor. We are not advocating that you make contemporaneous notes of every interaction with your husband or note down every word your children say, but just those that are of importance. You will quickly learn what is significant. Usually it is when there are heightened emotions during the legal process, discord or a negative behavioural pattern emerging that you should be most concerned and when you should be documenting the most.

For example, if your husband starts texting you about a matter incessantly or obsessively, is aggressive or abusive on the phone to you or your children, or if your children are coming home after contact with their father expressing stress or distress – make a note – and add details of the conversation. We don't suggest you inform your solicitor (keep the costs in mind here) or anyone else with the minutiae of what may be going on every day. However, these notes will assist you in having meaningful conversations with your solicitor – which are supported by fact. As with everything, facts and the truth are vital. This is a way of not dealing in pure emotion and when you are dealing with matters relating to the children it is of even greater importance.

These notes will perform two vital functions. Firstly,

they enable you to recall facts accurately and coherently. Judges look for reliability and credibility in a witness and will assess those qualities by reference to your accuracy and consistency when recalling events. With all the other pressures on you, you may well not be able to remember specific times and dates after several months or even years, particularly when upset. A note made at the time can be a godsend when you are being challenged by the other side's lawyer.

Secondly, they save you money. In any dispute, much of the lawyer's time with the client (and hence the fees) is built up trying to establish a factual framework of evidence: what happened, when, where – who was there? What happened in what order? Who said what to whom? A client who spends hours fumbling for the facts amidst floods of tears and ends up telling the story three different ways is wasting money – and is likely to leave her solicitor feeling apprehensive as to how she will come across in court.

Courts are not impressed by emotional outbursts. Judges generally don't want to know in detail how you feel – they are not unsympathetic but they want the facts.

EMAIL TO SELF

A simple method of recording information is to email yourself. Title each email in the same way every time so that you can easily search and collate them in a mail folder in date order. This means that the communication with 'yourself' is date stamped. Texts can be copied and pasted into an email to yourself. Here you will need to record the time of the text if there is a series or a conversation – the date stamp may not be sufficient. This method allows you to take action, keep a record and set aside an incident that may have been upsetting and distracting.

Refer to Chapter Four on communication for tips on how to respond to communiqués from your husband on a series of matters and how to avoid escalating a situation or being drawn into conversations or exchanges you do not want to have.

SET UP A DIVORCE DIARY

Get a day book. Don't use pieces of paper, Post-it notes or the back of your online grocery receipt. The day book becomes a vehicle of action, somewhere to jot down notes, the key decisions you need to make and the questions you need to ask your lawyer or other key stakeholders in the process (your children, the bank manager, etc.). Your actions lists on a day-to-day basis may be quite extensive during certain periods of the process. And all of this is over and above your 'day job'…that of being a mother, a friend, work colleague, boss, etc. You will need to be disciplined and religious in your approach to this.

Work from the back of the book when noting down your wildest and angriest thoughts and express your frustrations as copiously as you can. It is better to do this in a notebook than to offload to a friend at the school gate, a work colleague, your lawyer – or even worse your soon to be ex-husband!

We know that you may receive a call or an irritating text message from your ex, or perhaps a question for your lawyer might pop into your head whilst you're changing a nappy or stuck in traffic. You will feel much better for having written the important point down and it will satisfy your need for immediate action. The book provides you with a place to set something down, then you can come back to it when you are in the right frame of mind to think about it. It will also ensure that you minimize time with your solicitor when you next have a call or meeting. You could send yourself an email but the physical action of writing something down and being able to put it in a drawer is something that an email to yourself cannot achieve.

CHAPTER FOUR

Communication

'Whatever words we utter should be chosen with care for people will hear them and be influenced by them for good or ill.'

Buddha

MANAGING COMMUNICATION

We live in a world where there is not only a great desire to communicate but also the technology with which to do it. It is probably not too much of an exaggeration to say that we are now on the verge of reaching the saturation point of 'over-communication'. We have become a society that is obsessed with being in touch, constantly connecting, and 'reaching out' to friends, family, colleagues, loose acquaintances – anyone, in fact, who will listen or give their attention for a split second. We email, we phone, we text, we Skype, we IM, we Facebook, we Twitter – instant upload, instant download – instant offload.

Who would have believed only five years ago that you could talk in real-time and have your moving image 'beamed' across the globe? The novelty factor is at best responsible for turning us into a nation obsessed with instant gratification and at worst of impacting on our privacy – or even our human rights. We genuinely never know when we are being filmed or recorded – whether it be CCTV or even inadvertently in our own homes, by our very own children who are 'face-timing' their friends – or even their father, your ex. It can be like having a spy in your very own home – and such invasion of privacy is only going to get worse.

As you are going through the divorce process there will be times when you need to speak to people, to share your feelings and ask advice. One of the keys to this is managing the flow of communication, choosing the right person to speak to and picking the right moment to do it.

PAUSE AND THINK

It is always best to treat any communication with caution when you are in the process of getting divorced. In Chapter One we explored how, in the early days, you will be the most 'interesting' person in your social group, in the office or at the school gate. The more acrimonious, the more random and the more extreme the stories, the greater the level of entertainment for the listener – and you do not want to become a side show. Some will nod sympathetically as you tell them the story of your ex-partner having you followed by a private detective (something that happens a great deal more in divorces than you might imagine – private eyes are cheap and easy to find). The listener may think you are imagining things, fabricating, exaggerating – or even lying. So be careful. The more outlandish the scenario you are about to impart, the more important it is to pause and think.

There is also the very real risk that what you are sharing could be twisted, re-told with 'embellishments' or even used as evidence in your divorce proceedings by your ex. For example, you might be out socializing too much, or leave the children with a babysitter too often when you are out at work. Whatever the story, it is not worth the 'fallout'. In an acrimonious divorce your partner could even bring up at court something that never happened, or you never said – or something that he 'heard on the grape-vine' through parents at school.

By no means are we saying that you should not share your concerns, difficulties, extraordinary experiences or frustrations – but just choose someone who really cares about you. It really is vital to unburden yourself or you are on the rocky road to depression and isolation.

REASSESS YOUR CIRCLE

Work out who you can trust based on their track-record and your intuition; in addition, think carefully about what details you are prepared to trust them with. There is no harm in chatting 'broadly' about what's going on, but remember you are in a situation that is affecting those close to you, your family and your children. Stop and think and do not feel guilty about your newfound 'observational detachment'. This is a time in your life when it is essential to put yourself first, which is not something that most women are very good at. Anyone who really has your best interests at heart will understand.

It is very easy to get drawn into conversations. For example, picture the scenario where an acquaintance or your lawyer calls immediately after you have had a heated conversation with your partner: you're stressed and angry and so you let rip. You may as well prepare yourself for the fact that there will be times when your emotions simply take over or you need to work through and make sense of what you are feeling – but if you unburden yourself to your lawyer it will cost you handsomely – typically at a pre-agreed rate for every six-minute 'chunk' of time in which you are venting your emotions. Solicitors have to complete 'time-sheets' every day for their firms and virtually every minute of their day has to be accounted for – and billed accordingly. It is a luxury that few of us can afford.

If, however, you are unburdening yourself to an acquaintance, you can bet your last piece of misinformation that they will share it with others – and shockingly quickly. They will probably pass it onto the very next person they speak to: 'You'll never guess who I just spoke to…!'

And so the gossip begins. Get used to it. Robin Dunbar, an evolutionary biologist, found that gossiping aids social bonding – it's a kind of primitive co-dependency: 'I'll scratch your back if you scratch mine'. Sharing information can and has saved lives for as long as man has walked on earth – it is well and truly hardwired into our psyches. Ironically, the evidence is that gossips are seen as less trustworthy after sharing gossip with others (Turner, 2003) but this is unlikely to give you any comfort when you discover that your dirty washing is now in the public domain.

Divorce is a technical and complex process and when you speak to others about it you will almost certainly edit your story (as you will have absorbed the background detail and you will know the subject well). As a result, some may not 'get' or understand the true and full story and so may fill in the gaps themselves – inevitably colouring the picture or, worse, filling in the gaps with judgement and personal slant.

So if you are in a stressful or difficult spot it is always best to say 'I'll get back to you'.

LOOKING OUTSIDE YOUR CIRCLE

If unburdening yourself to a real friend is not possible or is not sufficient because of the strength of your emotions, then our advice is to find a good counsellor. Your GP can refer you to one free of charge on the NHS but there is usually a long waiting list. Alternatively, your GP can recommend a private counsellor but this can cost you anything between about £40 and £100 per hour. You can also find a local counsellor by visiting the British Association of Counselling and Psychotherapy (BACP) register at: www. bacp.co.uk.

It is still cheaper than unburdening yourself to your solicitor – who, in any event, is not qualified to deal with your emotions – just the technical details of your divorce. In fact, a good solicitor will probably point this out to you – or even give you the name of a counsellor. If they are experienced and have been practising family law for a long time, you can rest assured that they will have seen it all before. That is why we would advise against appointing too young a solicitor – no matter how qualified they appear – because life experience undoubtedly plays a major part in their understanding of your divorce and how effectively they handle it. (See Chapter Three, 'Choosing a Solicitor'.)

It is vital, however, that you do not lose touch with or avoid people – especially close friends. Their support is paramount but do ensure that you are in the right frame of mind when talking to them. Stay close to those that love you and that care for you but continue to think of what you say, to whom – and when.

COMMUNICATION WITH YOUR EX

As we explored in Chapter One, emotions are undoubtedly amplified on both sides during the process of divorce. Things will be said and written in the heat of the moment.

Of course, you cannot always suppress your emotions and there will be many incidences where you will experience a wholly justifiable and legitimate reaction to your partner.

BUTTON IT

Always pause and take a deep breath! What is written in a text, email or letter can come back to haunt you when used as 'evidence' to illustrate your behaviour and state of mind through the courts. It may well be a one-off tirade of genuine frustration but it will colour the opinion of those whose opinion counts: the judge, the CAFCASS (court) officer, the counsel. Going beyond the boundaries of what is deemed appropriate in a court of law is something that is just not wise to do now. You will have to spend hours compensating for or justifying a text that you composed in a matter of seconds in a state of shock or upset. There will be times when frustration, anger, guilt and even hatred will make you act out of character and your outburst may have a more lasting impact and legacy than you could ever imagine. Never underestimate the damage that a knee-jerk reaction can do. Keep your emotions buttoned-up for a more suitable moment. We cannot emphasise this point too strongly.

When your ex calls, texts or emails, it will be disruptive. Be aware that it can and will throw you off-course. It will instantly affect your mood and your concentration and will stop you from focusing on what you are doing. The tone of the communication will clearly make a difference to how it makes you feel but such an intrusion can be especially difficult to manage if you are working and are surrounded by colleagues.

TAKE A BREAK

If there is a chance to remove yourself and take a break, do it – take an early lunch, go to the bank or pick up your dry-cleaning. We are not suggesting that you go for a long walk or sit paralysed with emotion on a park bench, brooding about what you are going to write as a stinging retort. A quick break is normally all it takes to break the cycle of emotion – and get back on track with your day.

It can be no less difficult if you are a stay-at-home mum, surrounded by your children. Go to the kitchen or up to your bedroom, take a few deep breaths and read the message quietly if you feel you *really* have to at that moment. Otherwise park the phone away from you and come back to it when you are free from your children. They will pick up on your vibes immediately. Dependent on their age, this can happen more quickly and at a more instinctive level than with your adult friends.

If you are with girlfriends in Starbucks it is probably not the best time to vent your frustration in their presence by texting an instant response. They may even 'egg you on' in a misguided effort to help you do this. But even the best of intentions will not assist you at this moment. We suggest that you **pause** now and talk to them about it later when you have had the opportunity to ground yourself again.

It is always best not to try to assimilate the content of a communication on the spot and make an immediate response – unless a very simple answer is required to a very simple question. You will find that straightforward questions and answers, once so easy to handle with your ex, now feel immensely difficult and strained. This is quite understandable – your emotions and fears are inevitably wrapped up in the questions – and the answers that you give.

You will need to be thoughtful and measured in *everything* that you write and say. Texts and instant messaging are particularly easy to misinterpret due to their shorthand nature, so where there is any doubt or ambiguity it is *always* worth asking for clarification. In the same way, a response that you send without due thought may well be taken out of context and this can have an adverse impact on your ongoing interaction with lawyers, your ex and even your friends.

TAKE HIS TEMPERATURE

The divorce process will have multiple layers and levels of intensity. Measure the temperature of your relationship with your ex before responding and digest the true meaning of any request or message first. For your own sanity it is worth trying to take the intensity out of any communication. It is amazingly easy for a simple request to escalate into a heated argument or descend into mud-slinging. We are not proposing that you aspire to sainthood or manage to remain in total control all the time – but *pause before you press send*.

If your ex is sending you gross exaggerations or lies then these will need to be dealt with straightaway; but be certain that you are dealing in fact – not emotion. Do not go down the route of responding with equally awful things about your ex – even if you know they are true – it will serve no purpose. Anyone can twist a story or event to their advantage in divorce. So just PAUSE and think why or how you wish to respond. Clearly if there are critical things in the contents relating to your case or to any legal point it is sensible to discuss these with your lawyer. A method that worked for us is to write down your first reaction – get it off your chest then save it under 'what I really want to say' and park it. Then come back to it later at a moment when you have time to read it again properly. Only then send it, if you still think it is the right response. More often than not, you will not send the first anger-fuelled draft – but will give yourself the opportunity to re-work it into something that might just help diffuse the situation.

There are three main areas where you will have to interact with your partner:

- Children
- Money
- Each other's behaviour and responsibilities

FORMS OF COMMUNICATION FROM YOUR EX

- An ask – These can be official or informal but they are usually relatively unemotional. Perversely, if you receive a very matter-of-fact or 'cold' communication it can stir up emotions – especially if it is to do with children or relationships. This normally only happens when one of the parties is still 'in love' with the other.

- A tirade of anger, criticism or verbal abuse – Do NOT respond with an equally emotionally charged communication. This *never* helps although the temptation can be hard to resist. Your fingers will be positively itching to respond to something you have found intensely irritating. This is the time to draft and save! You may have raging opinions on how he cares for the children, about the way he introduces a new partner – or is generally irresponsible. You will have to calculate what is best in the circumstances and send a measured response, accordingly. It can feel as though having to behave like a grown-up has never been harder.

- The charm offensive – This is usually a reaction from him to a legal element coming to the fore. Perhaps you or he have changed your mind about something or reneged on a previous agreement. These communications are designed to appeal to your better nature and are often delivered with an ulterior motive. If he is pleading with you about something that is not part of the legal process then you have to decide whether it is even worth attempting a response. If, however, it is specifically related to the legal process and is clearly designed to sway you, then we would always advise you to consult your lawyer.

Points to Consider When Looking at Communications:

- Ensure you know what is being asked of you and ask for clarification before responding or making a decision. Don't respond until you are in the right place (not on a packed commuter train or in the supermarket!) and in the right frame of mind. If in doubt – don't!

- Ask yourself, 'Do I have to respond to this communication at all?' Sometimes it can be best just to ignore it. Or simply respond: 'Noted.' You have acknowledged the communication, you have taken action – and you can now park it. You can comfort yourself with the fact that this is how some members of the royal family respond to letters from inmates of mental institutions! If you do not feel that a response is warranted, then do not respond. This works particularly well for a tirade of emotion or anything that is irrational or abusive.

- If it is genuine (and you are able to distinguish that it is so), then considering what the reasons might be behind the 'pleading' message is a good thing to do. Could it be a reaction to a legal wrangle or a current issue of contention in the process, for example? Do take care not to make decisions without consulting your lawyer if the message is clearly designed to cajole you into agreeing to something. Also bear in mind that your ex will try to bargain with you – to your detriment. A typical example of this is with money and assets – furniture or cars, etc. In cases that are particularly protracted, such 'bargaining' could be considered a valid trade-off *if* you can come to an agreement and manage to look to the long-term gains.

- Be sure to watch out for abusive emails from your ex headed: 'Without Prejudice'. This is a particularly nasty and underhand method that some exes use to try to intimidate you and keep you in your place. The phrase is often misinterpreted by laymen as meaning that he can say anything that he likes, bully you, insult you, abuse you – and *none of it* will be permissible as evidence in court as long as the magic words appear at the top of the page. WRONG! 'Without Prejudice' applies *only* to prevent disclosure of communications made with a view to settlement. It ceases to apply once an agreement is reached. We would suggest that you acknowledge such emails with 'noted', collate them and let your solicitor see them at your next meeting.

HOW TO DEAL WITH INTRUSIVE COMMUNICATIONS FROM YOUR EX

It is very hard not to let your ex 'get to you' and disrupt your life on a regular basis. If your partner is controlling or abusive, they will use email, voicemail, letters and texts at any time of day or night to try to derail you and regain control over you. You must therefore ensure that you put measures in place as soon as possible that will allow you to take back control over your life and put a stop to the intermittent disruption and upset that such communications can generate.

Set up a new personal email account – one whose address you give *only* to your ex-partner. Inform him that you are doing this in order that his expectations are set early on. Let him know that you will respond to his emails – but not instantly – and only when it is convenient for you. If you are working and your partner knows your work email address, ask your company IT department to 'block' your partner's email address. This will prevent personal emails being sent to you during your working day. Be sure to think of aliases he might have that might slip through the IT 'net'. This will enable you to review his emails in your own time and help you to maintain a level of equilibrium in your day. This is one of the most valuable things that you can do early on in the divorce process.

It is almost impossible to prevent calls and texts, however, as we all need to retain our phone numbers for work, children, friends and family. If you have a private mobile as well as a business one you should consider changing your business number so that you can ignore personal texts until you are out of the office. This is clearly not ideal. The only way forward is to be strong and resilient. When he calls, let it switch over to voicemail and pick up the message when you are ready to attend to it.

With texts and IM, however, it is usually best to acknowledge receipt and say that you will get back to him. If you do not do this it might incite your partner into sending incessant texts that demand an immediate response.

A friend of ours who had a very controlling partner used to receive anything up to twenty texts a day at all times of the day and night. The friend explained that the increased frequency of texts, emails and calls used to coincide with times when the ex was asking her for a favour or her consent to a change in arrangements. These were *always* for the benefit of her ex and thus had little or no bearing on her own life at all. Such behaviour can become overwhelming and whilst you can try to remain detached, it is almost impossible not to get drawn into this kind of intensive bombardment.

We are in no way advocating any restriction of communication between your ex and your children. Whatever the state of your personal relationship, you will need to maintain your children's contact with him in most divorces – however acrimonious. In Chapter Eight, 'Contact and Residence', we will cover the 'why' and the 'what if' scenarios where indirect contact may be affected.

A Scenario

Your ex is supposed to have the children over the weekend, from midday on Saturday to Sunday afternoon. You have made plans for the weekend: lunch on Saturday and an afternoon with friends. He texts at 7 p.m. on Friday:

Ex: Decided to have a break in hotel with girlfriend so can't pick up at noon tomorrow.

You: This has been arranged for weeks and I have made plans.

Ex: Well nothing I can do as we are already here.

You: Check out earlier?

Ex: No can't – busy week and we wanted to have a break before kids come over.

You: Nothing surprises me any more. You could have done this last weekend when you didn't have the kids at all. Clearly your girlfriend and a night away take priority over your kids.

Ex: It is only a few hours. Change your plans – easier for you.

You: How can you afford to do that? You haven't paid the maintenance in 2 months and you are claiming poverty?!! I am not changing my plans so pick them up at noon or not at all.

Ex: Are you denying me access to the children? You will be hearing from my lawyers. You have no right to stop me seeing my children.

You: Up to you…

Ex: Be careful – I can make life very difficult for you.

It is amazing how one request for a few hours' delay can result in both parties descending into an argument. It seems so obvious what is happening. In the space of eleven texts the contentious issues of money, contact with the children and lawyers have already been introduced.

Let's break this down. How would his opening gambit make you feel? Would you be annoyed about your ex 'mucking up' your plans? Would you feel (however ridiculous) jealousy over the new girlfriend being taken away for a 'mini-break'? (You haven't had a lie-in or time to yourself in months.) Or would you be angry that he is spending money on a weekend away when you are currently trying to settle your joint finances? We suspect that it would be a mixture of all the above.

It is easy to look at this conversation and realize where the triggers are as a textbook exercise. But in the heat of the moment it is very hard to control your instant responses. If this is the first time he has asked you to delay his pick-up and you are going to lunch with a girlfriend and you could re-arrange – then you *can* stop at line one. So the best response might be: 'Noted – confirm exact time for pick-up'. Conversation over.

However, this could be the fourth or fifth time that he has 'ambushed' you like this. The frustration and the disruption that this is likely to cause you can change your mood in a second. And this mood-change could last for the rest of the evening and well into the following morning. Dependent on the character of your ex, he could be doing this out of thoughtlessness to wind you up, to hurt you or just to ruin your plans – or all of the above. When an ex behaves like this, he is 'feeding-off' your response and *wants* a reaction from *you*. It is a way in which he can feel as if he has some control over you – even from afar – and some influence over the way you feel. And it can hurt.

The Bully Boy

If your partner is controlling or bullying then he will certainly revert to type and become threatening and aggressive as the conversation progresses – especially if he is not getting his own way. The best way to nullify a bully is to take away their ability to feed off your emotions and responses. Stop responding to him completely but be aware that this is unlikely to stop him if he is hell-bent on disrupting your life. Trying to project *his* emotions on to you is another way that he will try to manipulate you – however trivial his emotions may be.

You are still the one person he knows most about and he will know how to push all your buttons. You can bet your last unspoiled weekend that this conversation will be relayed to his new girlfriend and that you will be deemed 'unreasonable', 'hysterical', 'crazy', or worse. Not that you will care what she thinks but no one likes to be thought of as a difficult or unpleasant person.

Take a deep breath and pause. If necessary break off the conversation and say you will get back to him in half an hour.

If a new girlfriend is a permanent fixture in your ex's life then she will no doubt start to spend some substantial periods of time with your children. This may affect you on many levels. You will want to ascertain that the woman who will be *in loco parentis* for a few days a month is a respectable, conscientious and caring woman who has the best interests of your child at heart. At the same time you may want to 'bury your head in the sand' about the fact that she exists at all. It can be a very difficult and painful time at a period in your life when you are already very vulnerable. When you are in the throes of 'deep fog' it can be difficult to work through the ramifications of a new mother figure for your children – so be kind to yourself and talk it through with someone you trust.

Think how to keep your plans in place even if they need to change slightly. This is important. If your partner has direct contact rights this is absolutely the correct line to take – you must not stop him from seeing the children and if you have an order or legal agreement in place then this is also technically the correct way to proceed. However, you can see how this escalation in a simple text exchange has heightened tension.

UNCONSUMMATED GROUNDS AND DIATRIBES

The other way in which your ex will be required to communicate with you is via the courts. This will take the form of written statements. These can run to lengthy diatribes. In a contentious divorce you may find that your ex will dredge up the past to a staggering degree in order to furnish his case by divulging intimate or embarrassing stories as a way of humiliating, upsetting or aggravating you.

These stories might very well have no bearing on the case whatsoever and may be vastly twisted away from the truth. For example, in the final stages of a particularly bitter divorce, Eve received her ex's response to the court on the night before the final hearing. The response ran to some twenty sides of A4 and the document was littered with wildly false accusations that even included a reference to the fact that she liked to have sex with strangers in graveyards! He used this fabricated character assassination as evidence of her unreasonable behaviour and cited it as a reason for his having left the marriage. He called her 'sick' and 'vindictive' and used this as 'evidence' that she had alienated the children.

We were obviously intrigued to find out whether the tale of Eve's graveyard romping had any element of truth to it. The fact is that it did! Eve said that in her early twenties she had had sex with her long-term boyfriend in a graveyard. This was only apparent to them after the event as it was dark and there were no gravestones to be seen. Eve told her ex-husband this story as part of a 'Where's the weirdest place you've ever had sex?' conversation. And hers won!

On a serious note you can see how a story can be manipulated and taken completely out of context and there is very little you can do about it. This story was presented to Eve's solicitor, her barrister and the presiding judge at the final hearing. One can imagine how intensely embarrassing this would have been for Eve in court. However, when she spoke to her solicitor he put her mind at rest, saying that the judge would not look at such personal trivia in respect of the divorce.

I'LL TAKE THE HIGH ROAD AND YOU TAKE THE LOW ROAD

Remember that involving your solicitors over something like this will cost you a great deal of money. If it is at all possible, endeavour to work out the disagreement between yourselves without having to resort to your solicitor to do it for you. Always take the high moral ground wherever possible – it may feel very painful at the time – but you will never regret it and you can use it as evidence of your reasonableness further down the line should things get even more difficult.

One of our friends had a husband who actually specified that he wanted almost all their joint possessions during the division of assets. This included trivial and relatively worthless items such as black bins, cutlery, and even plants that he wanted to dig up from their garden. This was clearly more about making her life miserable than about the actual items involved but her solicitor advised her to agree to everything. The items were relatively easy and cheap to replace and to dispute his requests would have cost a great deal more in terms of time and legal fees. The key is to be brutally honest with yourself about what you genuinely love. If you chose an item such as a painting and it has emotional value then fight for it. If not, you are better off without it. For example, do you really want those champagne glasses that were a wedding present? They will only remind you of him. Go out and buy some gorgeous new ones with which you can start to toast the happy moments in your new life.

Other points to consider:

- Facebook – In December 2009, Facebook was cited in 20 per cent of divorce cases as playing some part in the dissolution of a marriage and by December 2011 this figure had jumped to 33 per cent. The reason is clearly the ease with which individuals can post sexual or flirtatious comments in public view and as a result we strongly advise during your divorce that you refrain as much as possible from posting online anything that could be used as evidence against you in a court of law – however innocent or innocuous it may seem. This also applies to Twitter and Instagram.

- Written Correspondence – When it comes to writing emails we have already discussed the importance of setting up a personal email that is uniquely for your ex. This also allows you to keep a simple file of all interactions. It is best to put *everything in writing* as you will need an audit trail for some of the correspondence between you and your ex during your case. You may need to plan holidays, contact and maintenance. Email also helps to keep communication more formal, which can be useful when trying to negotiate incendiary issues like contact.

    Ensure that everything you write is factual. Don't respond emotionally to anything – it is a waste of your time and you do not want to share your feelings with your ex. Not only does this give him ammunition but it is a way of winding you up. Use your day book, as mentioned earlier, to offload your feelings and *be strong*. If you are also writing contemporaneous notes you can use these to support and evidence your negotiations and discussions.

Communication with your partner will at times seem debilitating and demoralizing. If your ex persists in using aggressive and unrelenting methods of communication, it can feel like a war of attrition and can make you feel under attack. Be strong, be strict with yourself – and *restrict* how much you communicate and respond. There is a reason you have appointed a lawyer!

PARTNER COMMUNICATION WITH YOUR CHILDREN OR FAMILY

It is clear that this is very dependent on the age of your children. Young children will find it very difficult to have a meaningful conversation with your ex over the phone – or with you if they are staying away from home. As a mother you will find this harder than you think. The little people that you see and speak to every day will not necessarily understand what you are saying over the phone – and may not even grasp where you are. Their conversation may well be monosyllabic and very short – a minute! This is normal. Bear in mind that it may *not* be because your partner is trying to stop them from speaking to you.

It can be frustrating and upsetting if your children are away for longer stretches of time. It is essential to know your ex-partner's landline, his mobile number and also the numbers of the children's carers or babysitters if relevant. It is best to arrange a time slot when you know you can reach them, as it can be very worrying to repeatedly leave messages when they are not returned.

If your child is away for just one night do think about whether it is essential to talk to them. You don't want to increase the tension any further. It is clearly dependent on whether your children are homesick – YOU are the best gauge of their emotions. So if your call might 'up the ante' then PAUSE before doing it.

If Skype is an option then this can help to make the

conversation more real for the children. However, Skype and Facetime can suffer from technical difficulties such as delays, and very small children can find it difficult to sit still.

We discuss in much more detail children and communication in Chapter Eight, 'Contact and Residence'.

CHAPTER FIVE

Extreme Divorce

'Fractures well cured make us more strong.'

Ralph Waldo Emerson

It is important to note that 'extreme divorce' is still far from being the norm – but it is nevertheless sufficiently serious when it does happen to warrant its own chapter. This chapter covers domestic violence, personality disorders, extreme behaviour, harassment, stalking and Post Traumatic Stress Disorder (PTSD). We also cover the options open to you to manage and counter such extreme circumstances, such as recourse to the police or the CPS, restraining orders and self-defence, and provide websites of services that are there to help you in an emergency.

DOMESTIC VIOLENCE – THE FACTS

It is a shocking but true fact that two women are killed every week in England and Wales at the hands of a partner or former partner. In fact, domestic violence affects one in four women at some point in their lives. Statistics can give no clue, however, to where it can happen – domestic violence crosses every social barrier and occurs in every culture, class and age group.

One in four women! Can you imagine if such colossal numbers of people were victims of terrorism or gang violence and such abominations were publicly manifested on a daily basis? The government would be forced to deploy the armed forces and the whole country would be in an uproar. But because it is a phenomenon that has no respect for social barriers and demographics and mostly occurs behind closed doors it is still considered a secret travesty – and as a result is almost completely taboo.

The police in the UK receive **one call from the public every minute** for assistance with domestic violence and an estimated 1,300 calls are received each day – or over 570,000 each year (Stanko, 2000) – the vast majority of which (89 per cent) are from women. So there is a very high likelihood that you, or someone close to you, will have been the victim of domestic violence. We know that it is not just women who are the victims – men also suffer at the hands of their partners – but since this is a guide for women we will only focus on what we – and other women close to us – have experienced.

And we have it on very good authority from people who work with victims of domestic violence that the figures are far greater in white middle-class England than ever makes the news. Domestic abusers aren't always heavily tattooed thugs with a pit bull. Spa towns in rural England are just as rife with domestic violence and it goes on in the households of judges, lawyers, doctors and executives. In these households it is even more taboo – because they have so much to lose and have so very far to fall. They are at risk of losing their social network, their incomes and their reputations. Little wonder that so few cases of it ever see the light of day.

WHAT IS DOMESTIC VIOLENCE?

It's important to realize that domestic violence (or alternatively domestic abuse) isn't limited to physical violence.

In law domestic violence is a pattern of coercive and controlling behaviour of violence or abuse including but not limited to psychological, physical, sexual, financial or emotional behaviour, which takes place within an intimate relationship (normally a co-habiting, family-type environment). It also includes forced marriages, 'honour' punishments and a wide range of abusive behaviour, not all of which are in themselves inherently 'violent' – such as harassing or controlling behaviour, financial control, bullying, throwing things or even spitting.

Abuse in the form of bullying and control creeps up in a most unsuspected way, the normalization of which happens without the victim perhaps even realizing it. The relentless nature of emotional abuse can become a subtext to everyday life and whilst you know it is not the right way to live, it can form a pattern and a series of learned behaviour on the parts of the victim and the perpetrator. One can hear the word 'sorry' being uttered by one half of the partnership daily whilst on the other the pleas or apologies are ignored. In this way you can be driven to believe that it is your fault and you are essentially useless. So you try harder to placate him and accept things in order to try to get the relationship back on track. The more you do this the more the cycle repeats itself and indeed speeds up the regularity of the incidents. Some can be as trivial as to what TV channel is watched – an abusive person will purposely choose channels you do not want to watch, act in a way they know irritates you, talk down to you in social situations and criticize the smallest things you do, even down to the ironing and cleaning. What appears a small matter in everyday life can become a cycle of behaviour and emotion that is nothing short of abuse.

Domestic violence can start very gradually and be a very occasional event, perhaps occurring once or twice a year over many years. You stay because things settle down and you may even see occasional glimpses of the man you married. He may apologize, shower you with bouquets of flowers and tell you how much he loves you – he may even appear to feel genuine remorse. (The more hard-bitten partners do not even make any attempt to do this). But then the intensity and the frequency of the incidents increase – and before you know it you are on the receiving end of regular and increasingly brutal treatment.

GETTING TO KNOW THE BOILED FROG

The famous 'boiled frog' metaphor is a good way to demonstrate how domestic violence can happen so insidiously. If you dropped a frog into a pan of boiling water it would leap out immediately – and save itself. But if you put the same frog into a pan of cold water and then heated it up very slowly to boiling point it would first become soporific and lose consciousness – and only much later die. The gradual, infinitely small gradations of temperature increase (or intensity) are the key here. The creeping, surreptitious nature of domestic violence is what makes it so lethal.

If you have been in an abusive relationship for any length of time at all it is beyond doubt that your self-esteem will be very low. You are likely to feel extremely depressed and ashamed about what is happening to you – even convince yourself that it is *your fault* that it is happening to you! Perhaps you think that something you have done has somehow caused him to behave in this way and it is extremely likely that he will try to convince you of this.

EXTREME BEHAVIOUR

SPITTING

'Spitting' is considered particularly relevant by various organizations (e.g. Relate) because it is generally the 'stepping stone' or linking action between non-violent and violent behaviour. It is a form of not-so-subtle conditioning or 'grooming' that habituates the victim over a period of time to expect (and accept) more and more extreme forms of abusive behaviour. If your partner has started to spit at you, it is time to get out of the relationship fast. It is a sign of contempt (see Chapter One, 'Preparing to Divorce' on the four behaviours that predict divorce) and **losing control**, and his conduct is likely to deteriorate into something much worse extremely quickly.

As a reasonable person in 'unchartered territory', it is perfectly understandable that you will feel a sense of shame but the reason why domestic violence does continue unabated for years is because the 'perpetrator' is aware of your sense of shame and is therefore confident in the knowledge that you are unlikely to report him to the police – or even tell your friends and family. He may even try to isolate you from your friends and family so that you do not tell them what is going on (see 'Narcissistic Personality Disorder', over).

According to Women's Aid (a national charity working to end violence against women and children), only a small minority of incidents of domestic violence are ever reported to the police, varying between 23 per cent (Walby and

Allen, 2004) and 35 per cent (Home Office, 2002). On average, there will have been **thirty-five incidents/assaults** before the police are called (Jaffe, 1982) but at some point (if a woman is still sufficiently strong) she may finally report it because what she has suffered is considerably more severe than previous assaults. Or she may at last wake up to the fact that she will not tolerate bringing up her children in such an environment. Not only is domestic abuse kept behind closed front doors, it is also kept behind bedroom doors out of the sight and hearing of the children, friends and family. Once this threshold is crossed, the whole charade often falls spectacularly apart.

STALKING

It is easy to think of stalking as something rather comical and harmless that is carried out by a man loitering on street corners in a dirty mackintosh. The reality is somewhat more sobering. According to the Home Office consultation report on stalking carried out in November 2011, one in twenty -five women aged 16–59 is a victim of stalking each year. One third of victims said that they had gone on to lose their jobs or their relationship or they had been forced to move because of stalking. It is a very serious phenomenon and destroys many lives. The Home Office definition of stalking is: 'two or more incidents causing distress, fear or alarm of obscene or threatening unwanted letters or phone calls, waiting or loitering around home or workplace, following or watching or interfering with or damaging personal property by any person including a partner or family member'.

The Protection from Harassment Act 1997 went some way towards affording victims protection but, in reality, it was difficult to prove and to police. Some 10,000 prosecutions were brought under the act in 2010, for example, and 85 per cent of offenders were prosecuted. Thirty-nine per cent of the perpetrators of stalking are partners or ex-partners and in 2012 The Protection of Freedoms Act was introduced in an attempt to close the gap in the prosecution rate by focusing on the **feelings of the victims and the harm caused to victims** rather than the components that constitute stalking. The Act created two new offences of stalking, including contacting someone by any means including via friends or online.

- 92 per cent of victims reported physical effects of anxiety, sleep disturbance, anger or Post Traumatic Stress Disorder.
- 50 per cent were forced to change their telephone number.
- 50 per cent were forced to give up social activities.
- 33 per cent were forced to relocate.

CHARACTER ASSASSINATION/HARASSMENT

Character assassination is harassment and it can take many forms: letters being written to you or to neighbours, friends, family, local officials; notices being pasted in public places; phone calls to third parties or postings on Facebook and Twitter. This is a blatant attempt to isolate you from your support network. This behaviour from your partner will make you feel desperately alone and further diminish your confidence. Ironically and bewilderingly, you may cling in isolated desperation to your abusive partner, which is well recognized in the Stockholm Syndrome. Unbelievably, this sort of psychological abuse can go on for years if your self-esteem is sufficiently diminished.

Character assassination is catastrophically undermining and devastating and if you have experienced it you will know how desperate it can make you feel. It is *vital* to report this to the police because with sufficient evidence (the writing is on the wall – sometimes literally) they can prosecute your partner and put in place a restraining order to prevent him from doing this again. In these circumstances, as with less serious manifestations of behaviour during acrimonious divorces, it is important that you deal in facts. Record events and behaviour patterns using the technique of contemporaneous notes (see page 60) and ensure that they deal with cause and effect and are date stamped. These notes will assist your lawyer and the police to have clear supporting information for any action.

ABUSIVE SOUP

Threats, harassment and intimidation are all forms of domestic abuse and if you are on the receiving end of any of these it can be horrific. It can feel as though your entire life is spiralling out of control. Don't waste time feeling sentimental for what once *was* – this is a very easy and common trap to fall into.

Wake up, get up and get out before you are simply too worn down to leave and before the surreal nature of what you are experiencing becomes normalized and you are terminally swimming in some kind of abusive soup. You can start again. Enlist the help of your friends and family – tell them what has been going on. Then it will no longer be taboo and the reaction of your friends should be sufficient to convince you that you are doing the right thing by leaving. No one should ever have to put up with such treatment.

CLAIRE'S LAW

Proactive measures are very slowly being undertaken to combat the rise in domestic violence. Claire's Law came into force in March 2014, enabling women to check their partners' history and find out whether they have ever been convicted of domestic violence.

Claire Wood met George Appleton on Facebook and was murdered by him in 2009 after she repeatedly reported him to the police. After her murder it was discovered that the police were aware that George Appleton had a history of harassment and threats to former partners. He committed suicide six days later.

If you have any doubts about a partner or ex-partner's behaviour – or about your safety – you are now legally entitled to know his history, so do not delay. Although you will feel extremely isolated, it is important to point out once again that you are not alone and that there are many support networks available to you. Never feel that you have no options and that you must stay. Even if you have no friends or family to turn to, there are shelters for women where you can go. Your doctor, social worker and social services are at hand, and you might also consider:

- Shelter: www.shelter.org.uk – Offers temporary and emergency accommodation, advocacy and support.
- Women's Aid: www.womensaid.org.uk
- National Centre for Domestic Violence – www.ncdv.org.uk – Offers free, fast emergency injunction advice and assistance service

There are always options open to us and it is important to remember this.

POLICE

Once you report an incident to the police they will *always* come out to you – even if it is many hours after the event. At the time you report it they will give you an incident number, which is the number of incidents that have happened on that day in your area. You must write this down so that if you need to call the police out again they will immediately be able to ascertain **who you are** and **how quickly they need to get out to you**.

Health Warning: It is somewhat disturbing to learn that the police will not always prosecute in some types of 'domestic disputes', even if you are already living separately from your husband but are not yet divorced. For example, if your husband were to break into your home and steal your belongings, the police would not prosecute unless there was clear evidence of an offence. The problem is in being able to prove that the items were yours and that he wasn't simply taking back his own possessions. If he has broken into the matrimonial home then he is also entirely entitled to do so from a legal standpoint unless the court has ordered him not to.

The police are not lawyers and will be reluctant to get involved in what is (to them) a 'grey area' of civil liability unless there is a clear breach of the criminal law, so you need to take every measure possible to ensure that you and your children are safe and not rely wholly on the police (see 'Changing Locks' under Chapter Two, 'Preparing your Child for Separation').

If you are separated from your ex and there has been a history of domestic violence, every time you call the police they will carry out a 'risk assessment' to discern your level of vulnerability so that they can then take steps to improve your safety, if necessary. The risk assessment is a form with a series of questions that you will need to grade by giving a number from one to five) to show how strongly you believe a statement to be true. For example, they will ask you how frightened you are of your ex, whether he has ever threatened to kill you (or himself), has ever used a weapon against you, whether he drinks heavily, takes prescription or other drugs or has ever been cruel to animals (a good indication of the potential for domestic violence). Other indicators of potential violence include whether your partner has financial problems, whether there is a dispute over contact with your children and whether or not he has made threats to you in the past.

If, as a result of carrying out the risk assessment, the police decide that they need to take steps to improve your safety (and that of your children) they will send a security team to your house to see what security improvements can be made. They may install new internal and external locks, sensors and security lights, block up your letterbox, install a panic alarm or, in really extreme cases, a safe room. This is a room that the police will make as secure as possible so that in the event that your ex breaks into your home, there is a room that will be very difficult to breach and **which will afford you extra time until the police arrive.** Examples of extreme measures are putting a metal skin on a door so that even fire cannot breach it.

Other measures that you can take yourself include installing CCTV cameras, although this can be expensive. It might well prove a good investment, however, if footage can be used as evidence in court.

CROWN PROSECUTION SERVICE

The CPS states on its website and in all its literature that it will *always* prosecute someone for domestic violence where they have been given sufficient evidence by the police. Even if the victim decides not to give evidence and prosecute, the CPS may well decide to prosecute anyway if it is considered to be in the public interest – but the chance of a successful prosecution is inevitably reduced. They use recorded 999 calls, accounts from police officers and any evidence they may have from call-outs.

It is really important to remember that according to the CPS, **domestic violence *always gets worse*.** In other words, leopards don't change their spots. Just take a moment to think about it. If your husband has hit you or has started to control you or bully you, the situation is never going to get better – **it will only deteriorate.** The fact that he has done it more than once proves that he thinks that he can get away with it again. You are living in a fantasy world if you think anything is going to change. It can be devastating when you come to this realization and it may take some time to sink in. Once it has, however, it should be sufficient incentive to get out of your marriage as quickly as possible.

Once you have reported an incident, and depending on the severity and nature of the situation, the police will inform various networks who will contact you to see how they can support you. You may be allocated an Independent Domestic Violence Advisor (IDVA) who will contact you regularly, support you and help to liaise between you and the police. This can be very reassuring and can make you feel significantly less isolated and vulnerable.

One of the most important things to remember is that it is essential to report each and every incident to the police.

Obviously if it is a 999-call situation, the matter will be logged and followed up, but you must be religious about logging all incidents such as harassment, character assassination and any breaches of a restraining order etc., (by calling 101) because it will ensure that the police are updated about your situation at all times. For example, they may log your telephone number as a priority number, which means that if you call 999 and even if they are already on another emergency call you are the first person the police respond to – even diverting from another 999 call to get to you first.

RESTRAINING ORDERS

If your partner has committed a violent assault on you there are several routes that you can take to get an order in place.

If you have already appointed a solicitor, instruct them to apply for a **non-molestation injunction** on your behalf (a 'non-mol'). This can include orders that bar your ex from coming to or near the home. This will cost you anything from a few hundred pounds to about a thousand pounds. It is clearly not ideal if you are already short of funds. Consider borrowing money from a family member or friend if this is the case because nothing is more important than your safety. Remember that domestic violence situations are still covered by Legal Aid, so pursue this in the first instance. The National Centre for Domestic Violence provides help and guidance to getting an emergency injunction. They can refer you to a local solicitor and advise about eligibility for Legal Aid or provide a 'McKenzie friend' – someone who does not have to be legally qualified who can accompany you to court and assist in your proceedings. We have provided the contact details (see page 93).

Ask the police to pursue a prosecution through the CPS if they are not already actively pursuing it. This will entail going to court and giving evidence against your ex-partner. One of the reasons that domestic abuse was for many years not prosecuted was not, as is often suggested, that the police, the legal profession and the courts didn't take it seriously; it was that the police were wary of wasting time and money because the victim would frequently withdraw her complaint, refuse to give evidence or just not turn up at court to give evidence following pressure from the abuser and/or his family. Although this can be harrowing, a permanent restraining order following a conviction is free and is worth all the upset and anxiety to ensure that you are afforded some level of protection (under the Protection from Harassment Act 1997). With a permanent restraining order in place, the police will take your case more seriously should subsequent breaches occur and (because the facts have been proved to the higher criminal standard of proof, i.e., beyond reasonable doubt) they cannot be later challenged in civil proceedings in the Family Court. This can be extremely helpful, for example, in future hearings about the children.

Other Points to Consider:

- Occupation order – This is an order which grants one party the right to personally occupy the matrimonial home.
- Keep a diary – We cannot over-emphasise this. Most of the costs involved in 'non-mols' are to do with gathering evidence. If you have been keeping a detailed account of each and every incident it is very difficult for an abuser to deny or dismiss and easier for a judge to justify granting the application. You cannot make this stuff up!

- Self-defence: Flee or Fight – If your situation is extreme and your ex-partner poses a very real physical threat to you it is worth investigating self-defence classes such as karate. Not only does this make you aware of those around you and your personal space but it increases your confidence dramatically. Nothing is more liberating than feeling that you can defend yourself or make a pre-emptive strike if necessary. You will find that your whole attitude changes and that you can access internalized anger and channel this positively. Taking a course with a professional tutor will take time and application on your part but will be worthwhile. It will strike you as most unnatural but needs to be an essential change of mind-set. The added bonus here is that any of the martial arts will get you fit extremely quickly. We recommend any of the following self-defence martial arts: judo, karate, kick-boxing, aikido, ju-jitsu.
- In extreme cases it is also worth considering finding yourself a bodyguard or someone with a holistic view of self-defence who can talk you through the theory of assailant–victim mentality. They can also carry out a safety check at your home to identify vulnerable points if this has not already been done.
- Personal Audit – If you are genuinely at risk of a break-in by your ex-partner, you should do a personal audit of your day-to-day activities and how they might make you vulnerable. Such advice that might be given in an extreme case: if you are on sleeping pills you must come off them as you would not stand a chance of defending yourself if you came under assault in the middle of the night.

PERSONALITY DISORDERS

Personality disorders are particularly relevant to extreme divorce cases because they are likely to be at the root of the extreme behaviour that has forced you to flee your marriage.

The key elements of a personality disorder can be defined as long-term, rigid patterns of thinking and behaviour and it is somewhat surprising to learn that almost 5 per cent of people in the UK have some kind of personality disorder.

OBSESSIVE COMPULSIVE DISORDER (OCD)

OCD is the most common of the personality disorders and is suffered by 2 per cent of the population.

BORDERLINE PERSONALITY DISORDER (BPD)

BPD affects between and 1 and 2 per cent of the population and manifests as a tendency to act impulsively and without consideration to the consequences.

NARCISSISTIC PERSONALITY DISORDER (NPD)

NPD affects around 1 per cent of the population (of which the vast majority are men), but it is nevertheless of paramount significance. If you are in an abusive relationship, it is more than likely that your partner will be a Narcissist.

It can turn your life upside down to be involved with, or married to a narcissist, and you will almost certainly go away sadder or madder as a result of your relationship with them. Indeed, there is a high rate of suicide in victims of narcissists. Psychologists believe that narcissists have been emotionally abused as children so that they have been forced to develop a 'larger-than-life' personality built out of fantasies of unlimited success, power, brilliance – and even themselves as idealized lovers – and that is why the courtship with a narcissist is nearly always fast, heady and romantic in a rather obvious and public way. There will be lots of dinners out at very expensive restaurants, enormous bouquets sent to your workplace (so that others can see how much money he is spending on you) and excesses of every kind.

And that is the key to narcissism. The whole deal is about image – how they – and you – appear to the outside world. Once he has married you, the reality changes fast. There is no need to be nice to you since he has 'got you' and doesn't need to try any more. The expensive gifts and the charm will dry up as quickly as raindrops in the tropics and you will be left wondering what happened to the man that you adored and set above all others. It can be absolutely devastating to realize that your whole relationship was founded on their fantasy and needs alone – and that you were playing a role actually defined and scripted by them. They have an enormous sense of 'entitlement', which means that they believe they are entitled to the very best in life – without actually having to work for it or prove their worth. They truly believe that they are 'better' than everyone else.

Narcissists are self-obsessed bullies and they can be very cruel and vindictive when you 'step out of line', criticize them in a real or even a perceived way, or have any ambitions of your own that do not exactly match theirs.

They are often envious of others – or believe that others are envious of *them*. They create support networks that consist of a 'chosen few'. They will often marry women much younger than themselves so that they can control and dominate them. One real watershed in relationships with them is when children come along. Frequently, that is the moment at which the relationship flounders. The cause is that they are no longer the absolute focus of your attention. You naturally become re-focused and energized by your children, their needs and wants. In parallel your increase in power and confidence will irritate and inflame their animosity towards you.

Their need for admiration is so great that they will fabricate and embellish their own achievements – at the same time as continually devaluing yours. But the one distinguishing factor about NPD is that they have no empathy at all. They genuinely cannot understand why you might still be upset three months after a close family member has died or when *they* have had a ridiculous screaming match with one of your close friends. And they will not tolerate you being ill – because they need *your* full attention and *your* care and if you cannot give these you are redundant.

Narcissists are almost always charming, superficially charismatic men. They often rise seamlessly to the top of their profession because people mistake their confidence and swagger for leadership qualities. However, this rise to power can be built – just like their relationships – on very unstable foundations. They change jobs with great regularity because they have such difficulty working for, or with, other people. They frequently have their own businesses because they recognize that in a more open corporate environment they will be exposed.

One of the biggest giveaways is that narcissists contradict themselves constantly. They lie – a lot. They are even capable of lying about *facts* and things that you have told *them* and will accuse you of going crazy when you object. This is because they often project their own emotions onto you and then accuse you of something that they have done – or feel. They are capable of extreme cruelty, which is why relationships with narcissists so often end in violence.

Narcissists are particularly prone to lengthy contact disputes. Unlike divorce proceedings they can keep these going for years. It is a way of enforcing control. They can always invent things! Unfortunately for them, narcissists do not do well in court because they lie a lot and don't remember what they have said to judges. This is how judges frequently catch them out. Therefore keeping a diary is your best weapon.

POST TRAUMATIC STRESS DISORDER (PTSD)

PTSD is an anxiety disorder that follows one or more stressful events of a particularly threatening or cataclysmic kind. Acts of violence that are intentionally carried out are more likely to result in PTSD than are natural events. Symptoms include: flashbacks, phobias of places, panic attacks, sleep disturbances, or amnesia related to the event.

Symptoms usually develop immediately after the event but in less than 15 per cent of cases there will be a significant delay and sometimes it is years before someone will seek help but the good news is that less than a quarter of people who have experienced distressing psychological symptoms will remain permanently affected by them. Interestingly enough, women are more likely than men to experience more high-impact trauma and as a result are more likely to develop PTSD than men. Just over 8 per cent of men will experience PTSD compared with just over 20 per cent of women. Where children experience violence in the family setting, approximately 25 per cent will go on to develop PTSD.

Health warning: We have highlighted the very worst of what is possible in this chapter and you may experience degrees of this in your marriage. We want you to be aware of these but to not define any merely acrimonious behaviour as 'extreme'. Any manifestation of extreme behaviour will need detailed and robust evidence and clear, ongoing and long-term patterns.

CHAPTER SIX

Court Process

'Justice delayed is justice denied.'

William E. Gladstone

THE LAW OF GRAVITY

This is where the legal aspects of your divorce really kick in and where you may start to feel the full impact and gravity of your situation. Courts have a way of doing that to you! It is important that you are aware of what to expect because you will need to jump through several hoops – some of which will prove challenging and even bewildering.

The proceedings deal systematically with each stage of your divorce. Whilst initially you may think it will be straightforward, if your divorce is acrimonious or contested it will take much longer – possibly as long as eighteen months up to the point of Decree Nisi. We will explore the legal jargon and what it means later in this chapter.

Any confrontation is tough but this is exacerbated by the fact that this one is being conducted in a legal context and played out in a court room. What appears so dazzling and exciting on the TV does not remotely resemble the reality of your life now. If you are required to go to court for more serious contact and financial issues, the presence of a judge can seem as far away from a glamorous court drama as it is possible to get and it adds a layer of complexity and stress that you need to prepare yourself for.

Much of the divorce process is conducted without your attendance being necessary but there will be occasions when you will have to be present in court. When this happens remember the following:

- Be strong – our special mantra.
- Your ex will be nervous too – perhaps even more than you – men are sometimes just better at covering it up.
- Prepare yourself well: if you have been making contemporaneous notes these will be of enormous help in contextualizing any divorce petition or application to the court. These will not be used in their entirety and some points that you consider vital may not even be considered. Be guided by your solicitor and/or barrister. It is very easy to forget the objective of the hearing.
- It may help to visit the court a few days beforehand to explore, check the location of parking, toilets, etc. Family hearings are private, but there may well be civil trials going on before a District Judge, which are open to the public. The procedure is different, and they are in open court not in chambers, but you will get a feel for the way the judge and participants approach the process of a hearing.
- You will have time before the hearing with your lawyers so use this time wisely. You may only have an hour and you may think this is not enough time to discuss everything you need to *but it is*. Your lawyers come into their own here.
- When you are in the court, listen very hard. The formality of the language can throw you.
- You will probably not have to say anything directly to the judge. The judge may ask your counsel for clarification and he may

then ask you a question quietly – a bit like a theatrical aside – so you will need to listen, however distracted you are by the proceedings or seeing your ex.

- You will probably have the shakes! This is quite normal, even if your ex isn't there and you are confident of your case. Your stomach will churn and you will wish you hadn't had the quadruple espresso in the café before court. Staying awake will not be a problem...
- Being unemotional will be tough – but it is vital.
- It can be good to take someone along with you but be aware that it can be distracting. Some elements of the process will be for your eyes and ears only and you will need to focus on what your lawyers are saying in order to really understand what just went on. Sometimes you will be bewildered and will not fully comprehend the outcome or next steps. There may be technical procedures that you have not heard of before. It is also good to have space so that you can 'process the process' after the hearing before dissecting it with a friend or family.
- Make sure you get a good night's sleep. This may be impossible but do try nevertheless.
- Think about what you are going to wear. Looking good and being groomed will make you feel more confident. Look businesslike but not too austere. Arriving at court and finding you have a ladder in your tights or the remnants of little Johnny's breakfast down the front of your shirt is no way to feel relaxed.
- Be strong.

WHICH COURT?

Your case will be heard in the Family Court, probably where the petition was issued, which will be your local court if you are the one filing for divorce – although not all of them can deal with divorce. In the event that your case is sensitive or you are trying to avoid any local fallout, you may request that your case is heard in another part of the country (jurisdiction).

The vast majority of divorce cases, about both money and children, will be heard by a District Judge, who is called 'Sir' or 'Ma'am'. If the amounts involved run into millions, involve a significant foreign element or raise a difficult legal question, the case may be heard by a Circuit or even a High Court judge – but that is unusual.

There are a lot of misconceptions about judges and courts – in large part arising from television dramas and films, which almost always get it wrong. The District Judge will probably be aged between forty-five and sixty-five, though some are younger or older. They may well be female. They will be a former solicitor or barrister of many years' standing. They are probably married – perhaps divorced. They probably have children. They shop at Sainsbury's and go to parents' evenings. They might have a Coldplay album. They go to the gym, or play golf, or ride a motorcycle at weekends. In other words, they are no different from anyone else.

The hearings will usually be in private in the judge's chambers – a large room in which you sit at a table with the judge behind a desk. The judge won't generally wear a wig or robes and nor will the lawyers. The proceedings will be recorded.

Remember you are unique – but your situation, and the issues it raises are not. The court is very experienced in dealing with these sorts of cases. They will want to identify at an early stage what the actual issues are. They tend to be pragmatic, and appreciate brevity, realism, reasonableness and a willingness to contemplate negotiation.

They are not generally impressed by **histrionics**, shouting matches or a refusal even to contemplate that your view may not prevail.

In financial disputes, the procedure is designed to encourage the parties to talk and reach their own agreements whenever possible, and to reach a clean financial break if the parties' needs and assets allow. Legal advice and representation always helps. Beware those who tell you otherwise.

If your ex is earning much more than you or you are a mother at home, you will need to think in advance how you fund the proceedings. Remember that at the outset you do not know how long your divorce will take. Your lawyer can give you a guideline – but if you suspect a long struggle due to the nature of the relationship with your ex or your circumstances, budget for 25 per cent more for good measure. You can't, of course, legislate for every twist and turn but an element of flexibility will stand you in good stead.

Consider your funding options: do you have a legal expenses insurance bundle included in your home insurance and, if so, does it cover matrimonial breakdown?

Explore whether your solicitor will consider a 'no-win no-fee' option. It is unusual but nevertheless worth a try if there are substantial liquid assets that will need to be sold to pay you a lump sum as part of the overall settlement.

THE LAWYER'S BRAIN
My Dog's Bigger Than Yours

The *really* good lawyers aren't the overtly aggressive 'Rottweilers' – that's just to impress naive clients who confuse bark with bite. They are firm and determined – but not confrontational. The aim is to persuade the other side or, more importantly, the judge, that their client's argument is the right one.

My Lawyer Made Me Do It

Remember that telling the client what they *could* claim is one thing – but it's the client's decision to do it. Contrary to public perception, solicitors or barristers deliberately spinning out the dispute for a bigger fee is rare though it probably does happen – there are bad apples in every profession. What is much more common are the disgruntled parties who don't get or won't listen to advice, who insist on trying to do things 'their way' because they know best and who want to fight every issue, however pointless, or pursue a case that is doomed to fail, which of course drives up the bill without any help from the lawyers. They then blame the system and the lawyers.

If you are acting for yourself you may, if you want, ask to be accompanied by a 'McKenzie Friend' to offer advice and support, take notes, and generally help you – but they may not speak on your behalf.

- Prepare your papers beforehand. Make sure you have copies of all relevant documents in order in a binder so you can find them. Bring copies for the court and your opponent.
- Don't be afraid to talk to the other side's representatives before the hearing. This is normal – they are not trying to con you. Usually they want to see what, if anything, can be agreed beforehand.
- Always be frank and honest – credibility is key. Once you have lost credibility with a judge you can never get it back.

- Answer the question you're asked – not the one you would prefer to answer. Otherwise you may seem evasive.
- If you don't know or remember – say so. It's OK. The really bad mistake is to guess or invent something.
- And if you don't understand – ask. The judge isn't an ogre and is trying to ensure a 'level playing field'. You'll find that most opposing solicitors are actually fairly helpful in terms of procedure (if only because they want the case to proceed smoothly), although of course neither the judge nor your opponent can advise you on the actual issues in the case.

LEGAL JARGON

In most legal papers capital letters are used for the key nouns. This can seem alienating and intimidating, at a time when you most want to feel embraced by a 'caring' process. If you are the one filing for divorce (man or woman) you are called the **Petitioner** and your partner will be called the **Respondent**. However, if you are applying to court outside the formal divorce proceedings you will be called the **Applicant** and your ex will remain the **Respondent**. If you are the Petitioner for Divorce in the first instance – were your partner to apply to the court on a specific matter during the proceedings he would then be deemed to be the **Applicant**.

There is only one basis for divorce – that the marriage has irretrievably broken down – but that is established by proving one of five grounds (reasons):

A. Adultery
B. Unreasonable behaviour
C. Desertion

D. Separation for two years with the consent
of the other side
E. Separation for five years

The ground is stated in the divorce proceedings. In divorce
you can never petition jointly. As the Petitioner you are
likely to carry the burden of most court fees and legal costs
– however, it is reasonable to ask your ex to fund half of the
legal costs, particularly if petitioning on ground (D) – two
years' separation with consent.

CHEMICAL REACTION

When you are going through a break-up you can be open to
'suggestion' and can be über-conciliatory to keep arguments
to a minimum. Your ex may want to save on legal bills, may
have a new partner and want a 'fast out'. It is always good
to litmus test your ex's motives (and yours) and what stage
you are at. So watch out for signs of change in the progress
of your divorce if you are handling this yourself.

Even if your case appears undefended – i.e., you and
your ex have agreed matters in relation to your children
and the money **it is still wise to seek legal advice**. It will
cost you but could highlight some key points that you may
have missed. Use this time with a lawyer as insurance for
the future. In the event that things get more complex, you
can go back to the firm for further advice.

THE PETITION

The Courts Service cannot give legal advice but the website
has some useful Divorce Petition Notes for guidance at

www.justice.gov.uk. It is imperative you follow precisely the instructions contained in the D8 guide. If there are any mistakes or errors, you may find the judge will not grant the Decree Nisi. This will cause you no end of inconvenience and delay.

Step One
The Petitioner (you) will prepare a statement for the court, in conjunction with your solicitor if you have one.

Health warning: do read the explanatory guidance notes before committing pen to paper. It will broadly contain the aspects of your personal situation. In relation to your children or 'family', you will state facts such as if they are children of you both, adopted by both of you, stepchildren or other children that at any stage in your marriage can be deemed part of your family – however, this does not include foster children. Children fall into several categories and you must be precise: children under the age of eighteen and not in full-time education but over sixteen and in full-time employment or unemployed need to be included.

At the end of the court petition there is a section called a 'prayer', which is the formal request for the marriage to be ended (dissolved). In the event of unreasonable behaviour, adultery or desertion it is normal for the petition to ask for costs to be paid by the Respondent. You are very unlikely to get all your legal costs paid, so bear this in mind in relation to any further applications to the court.

In a section called 'financial remedies', orders for maintenance (called periodical payments) lump sum, pensions/ life insurance, asset divisions, property adjustments are listed. These are not detailed at this stage so you will not need to specify amounts.

Health Warning: if you have agreed with your ex not to have a financial claim against him at this stage, do not waive or cross out this section on the petition. If it is not included now you have no recourse to make a claim if circumstances change and the judge cannot rule to dismiss all claims as full and final settlement.

The petition will be signed by you and your lawyer's contact details will be inserted so that the court corresponds with them.

Step Two
The Petition and an Acknowledgement of Service form will be issued, checked and assigned a case number by the courts.

It is then sent by the court or, if you ask, your lawyers to your ex's lawyers (or him personally if he is representing himself). He should fill in and sign to say that he has been served and whether he intends to defend the proceedings, or dispute costs. He then sends it back to the court. The Petition is issued and then served. The only thing the Respondent may sign beforehand is a confession statement in adultery cases or consent in a two-year separation case.

Step Three
The Court will send a copy of the Respondent's completed service form to your solicitors.

Step Four
As the Petitioner you will then be asked to complete a form that will state that everything you have alleged is

true, and you will then ask for a date to be set for the Decree Nisi.

Step Five
The judge will fix a date for the Decree Nisi (conditional order) once he is satisfied that the documents are in order. The court will send this to both parties.

Step Six
The Decree Nisi is a very simple and rather unceremonious event. There is no need for you or your ex to attend court unless your claim for costs (if you made one) is defended – or if you are the Respondent defending a claim for costs. If so you *must* notify the court and the other side that you will be attending to challenge the claim for costs. If you don't do this the judge may well refuse to let you say anything. A court clerk will read out a list of surnames relating to those cases on the roll that day. The judge will make a short statement and pronounce all decrees. The decree will be sent out to all parties.

Step Seven
Precisely six weeks and one day after the Decree Nisi has been pronounced by the judge, you (the Petitioner) can apply to the court for the final decree – the **Decree Absolute**. You will need to complete a D36 form, which you will prepare with your lawyer. If you are representing yourself, the court will have the forms you need.

It is possible to reduce the time of six weeks and one day but you will need to make a formal application to the court. This would only be granted in a legitimate emergency or exceptional circumstance, for example if you needed to remarry before a child is born.

If you do not apply for the Decree Absolute, the Respondent can apply three months after the six weeks and one day has elapsed. A hearing date will then be set at which a decision will be made to consider the application.

Step Eight
A Decree Absolute or final order is the decree that ends your marriage.

FINANCIAL MATTERS
At any time from the issue of the petition you can initiate the financial remedy procedure *as long as you did not delete this from the petition*. It is often during this period that things start to heat up. There are several reasons for this: whether you like it or not you are now looking at the end, however long it has taken you both to get here, and old grievances may resurface. You are making key decisions around maintenance for you and your children and looking in granular detail at the division of assets, debts and pensions, etc. Also, disputes about contact and residence may be running in parallel with the financial dispute. Don't mix up the two, however tempting.

If you are struggling financially, this is the time when your ex can turn up the heat. You will have been fending on your own for some time financially – perhaps with the help of an interim arrangement that supports you and the children. In order to achieve the most favourable settlement for themselves, men (and women who want more than they first thought) can use this time to change the parameters of the settlement.

In a very acrimonious divorce a father may cut off some or all financial support in order to bring the divorce to a swifter conclusion. He may stop maintenance payments for the children in full or in part, cut off your maintenance and even stop paying the rent or mortgage on your residence with the children. This can leave you in a critical and dreadful position. Your home may even be at risk of being repossessed. Even if you are working, such a reduction in your income can have a massive impact.

When you get to 'the business end' of any negotiation it is normal for tactics to come into operation but such manoeuvres can be really unpleasant and disruptive. It will exert enormous pressure on you to move to a financial settlement more quickly and will add a layer of desperation to your life as you will be unable to secure funds for subsequent legal challenges/defence. Getting a loan is not an option if you are not working and if you have a property solely in your name you will not be able to raise funds from this as it will probably form part of your joint estate. Remortgaging the home you are living in will be impossible because the property will form part of the division of assets. As this division has not taken place, you will need your ex's signature for the transaction.

This all seems pretty straightforward but things can move very slowly when the agreement for full and final settlement is being negotiated.

Health Warning: it is important to know what properties are in your name (on the deeds). Even if your name is not on the land registry deeds, have you been contributing or even paying the mortgage? If so, investigate whether you need to put a charge over the properties to stop your ex selling them without your permission. This type of action will prevent this whilst proceedings are under way. This costs money so be sure that you have good reason to enforce this type of intervention. Always consult your lawyer.

APPLICATIONS TO THE COURT

Even in comparatively straightforward divorces, couples will have disagreements and you may need to seek the support of the legal system to carry on normal living. Maintenance Pending Suit is what will be paid (if the court so orders) before Decree Absolute. It is often called 'interim maintenance', and provides financial support for you or the children.

You cannot make an application to the court for a financial order until such time as the petition has been filed, and a final order in respect of the finances (except Maintenance Pending Suit) cannot take effect until the Decree Absolute has been awarded. Arrangements may be made by Decree Nisi and made an order at the time of Decree Absolute – however this is not always the case. After a Decree Absolute is pronounced by the judge, financial negotiations can still continue until the final order is made for full and final settlement.

The process for a financial order starts with you filling in **Form A**. Your lawyer will assist in completing this – all it means is that you intend to file a financial application. At this stage you do not have to submit any detailed information but the process speeds up now – so be prepared! Your lawyer will have briefed you on this. In approximately twelve to sixteen weeks you will need to have the First Appointment and a date will be set. (The purpose of this First Appointment is to find out what is needed to progress the case, allow you to air your issues and ensure you are following a process to minimize your costs.) You will then be sent a list of directions from the court and this, along with the Form A, should be sent to financial institutions and such organizations as pension providers.

Five weeks before the First Appointment date (thirty-five days to be precise) you will be required to prepare and submit **Form E** to the court and serve a copy on your ex – even if he hasn't done his. This form is VERY detailed and requires full disclosure. Any supporting documentation can be attached and it is advisable to do this. This disclosure is required by both parties. Any inaccuracy or procrastination will cause delays and further fees.

All the details of what is required will be shown on Form E.

Another document that forms part of this process is a statement from you about any issues and concerns that you might have. The court will also want to be informed about the length of your relationship, jobs, children and lifestyle, etc.

Once you have received you ex's Form E and he yours, you are allowed to ask for more information and greater clarity on details highlighted in the form by issuing a questionnaire.

It is very rare that you can or will be allowed to delay the First Appointment date so be prepared to complete the Form E. If you don't turn up then you will be liable for the costs incurred in wasting the court's time. So make sure you have done all your homework and planning around your diary well in advance. Give yourself some time either side of the hearing. It is stressful and intimidating and if you are confronting or seeing/speaking to your ex for the first time in ages (as you generally communicate only in respect of the children or over email) it can have a profound effect on you.

At the First Appointment you and your ex will both need to attend court. If you have been keeping contemporaneous notes along the way, you will much more easily be able to substantiate your case and any anomalies such as his lack of payments, etc.

FINANCIAL DISPUTE RESOLUTION

The judge will make directions (orders) that will address potentially expert witness input, valuations of property and the Financial Dispute Resolution (FDR) hearing. The judge may decide to adjourn or hold off the FDR until you and your partner have had a chance to mediate or negotiate away from the court.

Both of you will need to attend the FDR, and it will be up to you to reach an agreement. You need to demonstrate your acknowledgement and understanding of the fact that you have to make some changes and compromise.

It is an informal hearing and can take many hours so be prepared to be patient and flexible. It is very important that if in the intervening weeks you and your ex have exchanged any proposals relating to the case, that these are shared openly prior to the hearing. Some of these offers might have happened only the day before and may have missed the judge's bundle that morning. Do not worry too much about this as your lawyer is being paid to bring new evidence to light. Eleventh-hour submissions are not unusual in financial or contact disputes!

If you reach a deal (which is quite common), the judge will then issue an order covering the final terms that have been agreed. It is not unusual that an agreement is not reached at this stage but a deal is done shortly afterwards.

If not, the judge will make directions on any outstanding matters and list the case for a **final hearing** at which a different judge will decide the outcome.

HOW DOES THE COURT DECIDE WHAT FINANCIAL ORDERS TO MAKE?

The judge's first priority must always be, by law, to do what he or she thinks is in the best interests of any minor children of the family. After that, the other factors the court will bear in mind are set out in section 25 of the Matrimonial Causes Act 1973.

These are:

- The income, earning capacity, property and other financial resources which would be, in the opinion of the Court, reasonable to expect the parties of the marriage to take steps to acquire.
- Remember that Periodical Payments can be time limited. Be realistic about your future earning capacity. Are you currently working? Do you need to retrain? Can you increase your hours? How long do you think you will need to re-enter the workplace? How long has it been since you worked and has the market changed? Keep detailed records of suitable vacancies – or the lack of them – a few unsuccessful applications demonstrates that you have tried and are not just paying lip service to the idea of independence, which is a common argument raised in a settlement dispute.

- The financial needs, obligations and responsibilities that each of the parties to the marriage has or is likely to have in the foreseeable future.

- Financial needs are not the 'be all and end all' but they do tend to weigh heavily, all other things being equal. So calculate your financial needs and produce a realistic budget. Be prepared to back this up with invoices, receipts or figures. As you will have prepared a spreadsheet at the beginning of this process you will need to revisit this and thoroughly analyse what remains the same and what has changed. You will now have a realistic idea of your living expenses and costs for you and the children, especially if your divorce has been tricky and protracted. Bear in mind that as your children grow, the price of their clothing and shoes will increase. If you take them on holiday, flight costs and hotel supplements may also increase as they become teenagers. The best way to approach this is to keep a note of when and where the changes are taking place – transparency is key, both for your ex and ultimately for the court. If your children have finished full-time education, however, it will stop. We are not suggesting you unduly weight the figures in a bid to get more. Be generous but realistic – most people don't *need* six bedrooms, a tennis court or a fortnight in a catered chalet in Verbier. But be sure to substantiate what costs you do have. Keeping detailed records is an easy way to do this.

- Beware of taking 'soft' loans from your parents or friends. You will want the court to take these into account as a genuine liability and it is difficult to prove whether it is a loan or a gift. A written agreement, a record of the transfer of funds – not cash – and a firm repayment schedule all help.

- The standard of living enjoyed by the family before the breakdown of the marriage. Unfortunately, this is rarely helpful except in big-money cases – the cake can only be split so many ways.

- The age of each party to the marriage and the duration of the marriage: If you have lived together for a long time before getting married and perhaps a child or children were born while you were living together and you can demonstrate combined finances, then the time living together will be taken into consideration.

- Any physical or mental disability of either of the parties to the marriage.

- The contributions that each of the parties has made or is likely in the foreseeable future to make to the welfare of the family, including any contribution by looking after the home or caring for the family.

  The court's approach these days is to value monetary and non-monetary contributions equally. So staying at home to raise the children is regarded as equally valid a contribution as paying the mortgage.

- The conduct of each of the parties, if that conduct is such that it would, in the opinion of the Court, be inequitable to disregard it. Conduct is rarely taken into account unless it would be unfair to disregard it. It usually relates to financial irresponsibility or dishonesty or really extreme behaviour (such as serious violence). The court does not like historical slanging matches – or, indeed, mud-slinging. If your ex starts going on exotic holidays and has bought a new car while you are in the clapped-out jalopy and haven't had a holiday in eighteen months, this is rarely considered sufficiently serious to count as conduct (particularly post separation) although it may be highly relevant to the question of their resources!

  It is important to remember, however, that in a behaviour petition the Respondent is deemed to have admitted the allegations in the petition unless he expressly says otherwise.

This is a technical point but it is important to bear this in mind.

- In the case of proceedings for divorce or nullity of marriage, the value to each of the parties to the marriage of any benefit (for example, a pension) which by reason of dissolution or annulment of the marriage, that party will lose the chance of acquiring.

THE COURT'S POWERS

The Court can make a wide range of orders for periodical payments, lump sums, pension sharing and transfers of property. The Court's starting point is to attempt to achieve equality, but that is *only* a starting point and there is no one right answer. The Court must consider all the circumstances of the case and each one is different – or 'fact specific', as lawyers says. It is impossible for this book to give guidance as to what would be right in your case – so do make sure that you take advice from a qualified lawyer. (For applications to the court, see Chapter 8.)

MEDIATION

Mediation is the process of 'assisted negotiation'. It is often confused with 'arbitration' but the two are very different processes. An arbitrator (effectively a privately appointed judge) hears the case and imposes a decision. A mediator doesn't decide anything: they are a neutral intermediary who assists negotiation between the parties. While all good lawyers will be trying to broker a settlement anyway, a skilled mediator can sometimes make all the difference. Unfortunately the rate of take-up has declined sharply as more people act on their own behalf – either because they don't know what mediation is or how to embark on it or because they are unable to contemplate negotiation even through a third party. This is a shame because it is well worth pursuing. In the right cases it has a good success rate (Mediation only really works if both sides genuinely want to do a deal) and can be a very cost-effective way of reaching a settlement.

THE FUTURE

There are changes afoot under The Law Commission's new proposals to make it easier for people to negotiate their own financial settlement by using pre-calculated formulae. How that works in practice remains to be seen because of the wide variety of people's circumstances and the fact that it depends on everybody being fair – which is not always the case.

Pre-nuptial agreements may become legally binding in the future, which will give greater clarity and predictability on divorce. Whether this is at the expense of fairness remains to be seen. For example, how will the courts square the paramount aim of the children's welfare with an agreement that they and their mother are to have nothing on divorce except the clothes they stand up in? As always, the devil is in the detail and we shall have to see what, if any, safeguards are built into the system.

THINK LEPRECHAUN

All money matters are fact-sensitive and sometime just plain tricky between family and friends and these can become even more difficult when trying to separate emotional and financial issues. Pause before you launch into an aggressive dispute over money. Money is just money, so only fight for what you think is rightfully yours and what matters in terms of your financial security. And remember that the funds you expend fighting in the courts over money will dilute the golden pot at the end of the rainbow...

CHAPTER SEVEN

Working

'My work is the only ground I've ever had to stand on. To put it bluntly I seem to have a whole superstructure with no foundations. But I'm working on the foundations...'

Marilyn Monroe

THE REALITY

Working is a fact of life for most of us. And work is increasingly no longer a choice – no matter whether we are married, divorced or single. We need to and want to support our family financially. During divorce it is likely to become ever more critical and with the inevitable division of assets it is even more essential for us to become financially independent and to maximize the family income. To be a stay-at-home mum is a luxury that fewer and fewer of us can afford.

AND TO THE REAR, THE COMFORT ZONE

Juggling the demands of work and home will become even more exacting now that you are going through an acrimonious or prolonged divorce process. It becomes less of a work–life balance and more a full-time, unrelenting balancing act! During divorce the equation is not just about how much time you spend at work and how much time you spend with your children, but how you give your best in both environments. The pressure and stress can at times make your life feel exhausting, overwhelming and unachievable. And it will almost certainly make you feel as though you are stretching yourself way beyond your normal limits.

The real challenge is, of course, to do it all whilst remaining half sane! Divorce makes you question everything in your life on *every* level. This is where you will need to become a fabulous plate-spinner and juggler par excellence. You might even reflect that your work–life balance was poor enough when you were married and worry that it is going to now be impossible.

It is customarily repeated ad nauseam in the media that women did not achieve much by burning their bras in the female revolution of the fifties and sixties. Nevertheless, the outcome has been that we are more independent and can make our own choices about exactly how we live our lives. In a traditional sense, if you are a working mother the result is that you work in a relatively similar manner to any man doing the role but you are likely to *also* carry out most of the duties in and around the home. For the most part this includes organizing and managing the children, even when you are at work.

In the early days you may find that what seemed routine and easy when your partner was around now seems inexplicably more difficult. This may not be because you are doing more but because the breakdown of your relationship means that you are feeling the lack of emotional support. You are bound to feel vulnerable and exhausted. This is normal and it is essential at this point that you enlist the help of your family and friends. Explain to them how you are feeling – especially if you are struggling. Don't suffer in silence! It will take time to regain your equilibrium and it is a rare superwoman who can achieve this on her own.

It is likely that you will have already covered most of the practical elements – the childcare, school-run rota, day-care, babysitting and cleaning (or you may insist on doing it yourself – or have no choice in the matter). What will manifest itself now is the realization that it is now **all down to you** on a day-to-day basis. Sharing the unplanned changes and emergencies is suddenly much more challenging. If your child is sick and needs to be picked up at school, you are no longer able to call on your 'back-up'.

PRACTICAL OPTIONS

It really is worthwhile being proactive now and taking some time to explore your options. Is the answer simply to increase the hours of the nanny/childminder or day nursery? Is it a question of investigating after-school clubs for the children? Or are your parents/his parents or a close friend near enough to be able to step into the breach? As many families are scattered to the four corners of the country, this may not be an option. In the case of a family member or friend, if an emergency situation arises **make sure you have already had the conversation** with them and explain how things need to work. Think whether you are going to pay them and, if so, agree the amount per pick-up or overnight in advance. Your divorce could take several years and what may once or twice seem like a favour can turn into a regular burden – and even worse, you could be seen to be 'taking advantage'. Although they may resist payment in the beginning because they genuinely want to help, it will mean that you will have a clear conscience and that the **ground rules are clear from the start.** (For a family member the option could be to pay their petrol or they have their evening meal with you.)

Also bear in mind that if you are in Birmingham on work business and your children are in Kent and they are sick during the school day, it is not just a question of picking them up. It could mean a trip to the doctor's and a plethora of telephone calls. It is sensible to ensure that the school knows who is allowed to pick up the children and exactly whom they are allowed to leave the premises with. Do this in advance and then you will not be disturbed during a meeting by panicked school administrators trying to track you down.

This all sounds glaringly obvious, but failing to prepare yourself will have a *direct impact* on your ability to work. Prepare and prepare again. If your children are happy with the arrangements then you and they have peace of mind whilst you are away from them even on a normal working day. If you have some contingency plans in place then you know that you have an element of flexibility.

AND FULL STEAM AHEAD – THE GRAND CANYON

Divorce is monumentally distracting and there will be enough 'potholes' in your attention span relating to really serious matters without childcare arrangements adding to them. Your employer may allow you greater flexibility whilst you are going through the early stages of divorce but is likely to be less sympathetic if the situation is a recurring or prolonged one.

TOTAL DIARY MANAGEMENT (TDM)

TDM is the key to managing your work life and it is no coincidence that these letters sound like the word 'tedium'! It is easy to get into the trap of having the children's calendar on the fridge, a work diary on your laptop and perhaps even a personal calendar on an iPhone. We strongly advise that you have one schedule and only one – a master version. The way to make this meaningful is to colour code it. Choose one colour for your children's activities, one for your children's activities that you need to attend and one for your work or personal engagements. If you have a regular routine and work from home every Friday – move heaven and earth to keep it that way. Your routine helps to give the children's lives an established rhythm too.

We know this may sound über-obvious, but do be sure to write down the actual appointment times and if necessary the amount of travelling time you will need. If you work in several different offices then make a note of where you will be that day. One tiny slip is all it takes to bring the whole structure crashing down.

TAKE YOUR CHILDREN TO THE OFFICE

It is a good idea to let your children see where you work so that they can visualize where you spend time when you are away from them. Lots of companies have regular 'Bring your son or daughter to work' days. If the company has nothing like this in place then take them in on a quiet Friday afternoon – or even at the weekend.

BE WARY OF THE GORY STORY

It is always good to tell your employer about your changing circumstances so a meeting with your HR department and your direct manager is sometimes advisable. We are not suggesting you share the gory details but perhaps you need to make them aware that you will need to take time off to attend court and other legal meetings and there will be inevitable emergency childcare issues – now that you are the main carer for your children.

You must make it clear, however, that you do not see that this will unduly impact your work or your output for the company. In addition, however close you are to your HR department or line manager, the meeting must be conducted in a very professional manner. We do not recommend tears and overly emotional language. Keep it under wraps until you are back at home.

Most companies will show a clear understanding as divorce is common. Acrimonious and very protracted divorces are less common, so ensure you share only what is necessary and nothing more. Have an answer for 'So how do you see this affecting your work?' The answer to this is always: 'Not at all.'

WORKING FROM HOME

Another area worth exploring before your meeting with your HR and line manager is your company's policy on working from home. Find out what is needed to secure approval for it and what technology can be provided for you to be completely effective. Working off your iPhone and BlackBerry is not the answer. It is best to have an open conversation about this. You may already have an arrangement whereby you work from home one day a week. It might be possible to split this or add another day to your home-working. Do not feel as though you are asking an enormous 'favour'. It is in the interests of the company that you 'work smart' and working from home occasionally can be very productive and cost effective – so do not feel as though you are on the 'back foot' when you ask for this.

LOOSE TALK COSTS WIVES

It is inevitable that there will be casual conversations by the coffee machine or the photocopier. There may also be a frisson about the office and expect that gossip will be rife about your divorce for a while. Even if you consider work colleagues 'friends' and see them outside work, **don't get drawn into conversations and the detail surrounding you or your children.** All the good work with HR and your manager can be undone in a very short space of time.

An open office environment can cause problems. If you receive a call from your lawyer, your ex or a friend, don't take the call or, if you must, try to find a room or quiet area. It is always best to arrange calls with your lawyer via a conference call in your own time.

If you are speaking about your divorce in an open-plan environment, your colleagues will 'overhear' your conversation – even if they don't want to! No doubt the dramatic interlude will be far more interesting than their excel spreadsheet or the sales strategy for Patagonia. Also remember that a simple call can take on an emotional or even a heated turn. The last thing you need is a call that descends into a row. As you raise your voice or hiccup a sob, you will quickly realize that you urgently need to dash to the ladies' toilets to 'pull yourself together'. As you flee the office a well-meaning colleague (and there is always one) will see the tears welling up in your eyes and follow you as you run for cover. Then there will be a kindly inter-rogation, and no amount of saying that you are all right is likely to prevent this.

There are two potentially serious outcomes: they tell other people (including your boss) what they overheard or they tell people *and* make a judgement call that you are spending time in office hours handling your divorce – and are really taking the whole thing very badly. Neither of these outcomes is what you need or want.

If your ex has your work email address he may use this as a device to interrupt you or raise issues during your working day that you do not have the inclination or capacity to deal with there and then (see Chapter Four, 'Communication'). The best approach is to guide your partner to your newly set-up personal email address and deal with his communication when you have some clear time. If he persists, get in touch with your company IT department and ask them to block his name and aliases from coming in to your work inbox. We suggest you do not take calls from your ex in office hours – unless you are sure you can deal with it in an open office and that it will be a quick transactional call.

THE PRIDE, THE SANCTUARY AND THE GUILT

It really doesn't matter if you are married or divorcing, mothers always become wracked with guilt that they missed their daughter's performance as the Principal Slug in *The Plotters of Cabbage Patch Corner* or their son's summer concert when he had practised the violin so unrelentingly for weeks. It happens to all parents, not just mothers. We take it to heart and tear ourselves apart thinking that we should have been there. As a working mother, as long as you have told your child that you cannot make it in advance and the reasons for it, you will be amazed at how they will understand despite their obvious fleeting disappointment.

If their father is attending then this may not be such an issue for your children. But beware – experience shows that it will be noted by your partner that you weren't there and the ramifications could be he accuses you of prioritizing your work over the children. This is ridiculous but it will hurt, even if you know that it is the only event in the whole term you have missed. Sensible lawyers and judges see through such accusations. They know that you are playing a valued and supportive role financially, just as your partner is.

Younger children will notice when you are not around and may comment on this and you are bound to feel guilty. In fact, you may recognize that your routine has not really changed at all and that there have always been a few nights a month when you have worked very late.

Older children may not articulate this and the impact of you starting or continuing to work may not be so important. Nevertheless, it is really worth talking through why you are working and good for them to be aware of what you are doing and the ramifications. If you are the sole provider they should learn to respect and appreciate what you are doing and understand the efforts and impact your working has on the likelihood of them landing the new football strip at £40 a pop! They won't remember all the time. There will be times when they leave their dirty shirts in a heap on the floor and forget to let out the bath water. It can be hard coming home to a mess when you have had a killer of a day.

In every family, children of all ages should do jobs around the house occasionally. But at the time of divorce you have to be really careful not to use your work, long days and dreary commuter stories to make them feel guilty. And these types of conversations can spiral out of control to start touching on open wounds of the divorce. It can be really hard to keep it to yourself when you are breaking world records in keeping it all together.

THE UPSIDE

It can be a real boost to your self-confidence and sense of worth to be working successfully in your job. During divorce your self-confidence can be rocked to the very core. Many of us tend to imagine that if we are not the CEO of a massive corporation and earning a six-figure sum then it would not be worth getting out of bed for – but this is simply not the case in terms of the way it can make you feel to be holding down a demanding job. In addition, it can provide you with mental time-out from your divorce, which will impact positively on every other area of your life.

SLAP YOUR OWN BACK OCCASIONALLY

While you are in the process of trawling through emails or sitting in meetings whilst texting the childminder or the nanny under the conference-room table, take a moment to think: 'I really am doing all of this on my own. I really am contributing a huge amount and although juggling work and family is very hard, I am doing something enormously worthwhile in the best interests of my children.' This is even more valid if you are the sole or greater provider for your children.

YOUR INCOME

SOMETHING I PREPARED EARLIER

You may have shared a joint bank account with your ex but now is the time to look at your own income. You will have already prepared a spreadsheet for your lawyer to show the household and children's expenditure, which may or may not have included an increase in your need for childcare. You will need to demonstrate this now that you need more childcare as you are going back to work or are already working. It is important to prepare yourself for the fact that the work and money balance may well become an issue and a serious cause of contention with your ex.

TAX CREDITS AND WORKING TAX CREDITS

Explore whether you are eligible for these. According to the HMRC website:

- 'Tax credits are payments from the government. If you're responsible for at least one child or young person, you may qualify for Child Tax Credits. If you work, but are on a low income, you may qualify for Working Tax Credits. You can often get both types of tax credits. They aren't taxable.'
- http://www.hmrc.gov.uk/taxcredits/start/who-qualifies/what-are-taxcredits.htm
- 'Working Tax Credits is based on the hours you work and get paid for, or expect to be paid for. It doesn't matter if you're employed or self-employed, but unpaid work doesn't count as work when claiming tax credits. Check if your work can help you qualify for Working Tax Credits.' http://www.hmrc.gov.uk/taxcredits/start/whoqualifies/workingtaxcredit/work.htm

The links above are a good starting place.

CHECK YOUR TAX CODE

If you are already working, check your tax code. It is easy to fall into the trap of becoming 'laissez-faire' about such things when you are married. If you are starting a new job take a few moments to **check the tax code that your new employer puts you on.** It might be an emergency code – more than you should be paying or, even worse, less than you should be paying. In the latter event your tax bill will be a shock the following year and will cause some real financial hardship.

BEACHED 'WAIL' – DEBT MANAGEMENT

In this worst-case scenario, you will then have less income and potentially owe a large debt to the HMRC. They may be supportive if you contact them and willing to put a payment plan in place, but be realistic about what you can afford. This is not the time to find yourself financially 'beached'. You want to ensure that you retain a little flexibility.

Also make sure that you submit your tax online within the timeframe for Self-Assessment – there is a penalty of £100 for late submissions. And, as with all less than joyous tasks, it is inevitable that you will find yourself at midnight on 29 January rummaging through piles of bank statements, Sainsbury's receipts, carol service programmes (deadline being 31 January for online submission) trying to find your P11D. This is an annual event in many homes – so remember that you are not alone!

If you have your own business you may decide to appoint an accountant to do the groundwork on this but if you are an employee of a company then you should have all the necessary documentation to do it yourself. It is always worth asking a friend to help the first time – there is never any harm in learning the ropes from helpful friends. The good news is that it is usually straightforward.

The business environment is an ever-changing place and if you are venturing back to work or changing the way you work, it can provide a very flexible way of working. Contracts and freelancing may be good options to explore. The UK is a very mature environment for contracting and consulting. These types of roles are skill dependent, however, and certain industries are more accepting of this type of worker. We have included some websites to assist in the initial forays into these areas.

We assume that those of you who are freelancers or temporary workers will have existing arrangements in place – such as your own Limited company, Umbrella Company or Agency. If you are setting up for the first time as a contractor or consultant, then do ensure you take advice. Similarly, setting up a limited company can be tax efficient, but please take advice on this regarding your own personal circumstances.

Useful websites:
http://www.ukplc.com/.
https://www.gov.uk/business-legal-structures/overview
https://www.gov.uk/limited-company-formation/overview
www.hmrc.gov.uk/factsheet/limited-company
www.freelanceuk.com/become/set_up_freelance_company.shtml
http://www.myfdonline – a comparison site along with useful info on umbrella versus contracting.
www.workingmums.co.uk
http://www.e4s.co.uk/jobs/1-part-time-work-from-home-jobs.htm

If you are thinking of going back to work, some more progressive companies are looking at 'returning to work mothers' and genuinely provide for true home-working roles. The hours are typically very flexible (for example 10–3), which makes the school run possible and allows you to be with school-age children when they need you at home.

Remember, you will require reliable broadband to make this feasible. There are even roles that can support weekend and evening hours.

OVERSEAS TRAVEL AND MAKING PROVISION

Many of us have to travel for work – sometimes overseas – which certainly complicates the childcare arrangements and can become very costly. If your child's school has the option to board, then that might be a solution, but for most of us that is not an option. The first port of call has to be family and close friends – where with the latter it is likely that you will be able to pay back the favour at some point. Otherwise you are looking at paying someone to stay overnight in your home.

It is advisable to work out an arrangement with your normal childminder or nanny up front so there is no misunderstanding. For example, you might pay them the normal hourly babysitting rate until midnight and then pay again from 7 a.m. If your nanny lives in, this will not be an issue but ambiguity in the area of money always leads to resentment. You do not need the additional burden of having to start hiring new people to care for your children and, in any event, the opportunity to earn more money will be attractive to most.

If you have travelled a lot before your divorce and this now proves to be impossible because you do not want to leave your children or the costs are prohibitive, then you will need to have a frank and open conversation with your employer. Fortunately, the world abounds with technology provided by companies to reduce their travel budgets. Now is the time to leverage the technology to get you through this period of transition and establish alternative ways to work smart.

WORKING WITH YOUR EX – NO BUSINESS LIKE THE DIVORCE BUSINESS

There is another work scenario that is arguably more difficult than being the sole provider and that is to own and work for a company with your ex. It depends how the business is constructed. Are you a full-equity partner? Are you a director with fiduciary duties? Have you both jointly invested your collective money into the business? We can't cover every possible scenario in this book, but we are going to highlight a few areas you should be aware of and explore.

If you are an employee of your husband's company and you are not responsible for the payment of salaries and not a signatory for the company, we advise you to discuss with a lawyer what provisions you can make to ensure you are paid your salary on a regular basis. A formal legal undertaking may be all it takes to put this in place. Of course this doesn't prevent your ex from flagrantly flouting this, but you would then have recourse in the divorce/family court and not just through the labour tribunal/grievance process. The likelihood of your partner doing this is rare but he may use the business environment to increase the pressure on you if you are at a difficult phase of the divorce proceedings.

If you are a director of the company and have duties and legal accountability, then we strongly advise that you take legal advice from a specialist lawyer. If you have not been responsible for financial matters and are not intimate with the accounts of the firm it is important and your right and duty as a director that you fully appraise yourself of the accounts, future budgets and plans for the firm.

THE ELEPHANT HAS NOT YET LEFT THE PREMISES

Are you going to remain working for the company with your partner every day? Can you and your partner cope with this emotionally? What will be the impact to the business and your employees? You may start by thinking the situation can work but your working relationship can deteriorate shockingly quickly.

What are your options? You can leave or resign from your own company, but this may not be an option if you have money tied up in the funding of the business. You may be earning a good salary and it would be completely inequitable and unreasonable that you should be the one to leave.

Perhaps you are working for the same company and you just have to make it work. That might mean working from a different office if the company is big enough or, if practical, working from home more often to ensure the personal contact time is kept to a minimum.

'ARMAGEDDON OUT OF HERE'

In an extreme example of joint business, one of our contributors reported that her former partner systematically went out of his way to try to force her to resign. Tactics used included consistently not paying her salary coupled with non-payment of maintenance for the children, humiliating her in front of their joint staff and at board meetings and even campaigning over email to undermine all the work that she continued to carry out despite all the odds. She remained with the company for three further years and did so purely to support her children – and to cover the legal bills that poured in over the same period.

She explained to us that because of the complexity of the company structure and its finances she was concerned that if the company was in financial difficulty, she did not want, as its director, to be held legally accountable for the company and its staff. In return for complete indemnification in respect of all company matters, therefore, she gifted her partner her 50 per cent of the shares.

Her recommendation is that if you feel uncomfortable about the finances of your company for any reason, you should seek immediate legal advice. She recommends that if you have divorce lawyers, then use the same firm for your business affairs. This will save the endless briefing and re-briefing of lawyers and if you are dealing with a very difficult partner his behaviour on both sides of the case will inform the other.

This is obviously an extreme situation but she had no choice. The senior partner at the law firm she appointed gave her a piece of advice at their very first meeting: 'To achieve a happy, safe and secure future for you and your children you will have to be strong every day and focus on your end goal. Stay strong.'

And we can only echo that advice…

CHAPTER EIGHT

Contact and Residence

'Contact with a high-minded woman is good for the life of any man.'

Henry Vincent

Contact and Residence (formerly known as 'access' and 'custody') – what a hornet's nest of emotions these words provoke! This is where the divorce process becomes brutal, passions run high – and where someone *else* adjudicating from a detached and seemingly remote environment will be making the pivotal decisions as to how and when you will spend time with your *own* children. At times feelings are bound to spill over and you and your ex-partner may display irrational and exaggerated emotions (more than usual!). This bit of the process will rock your very foundations.

At this point it is important to be extra diligent, honest and aware of your own behaviour – and his. Ask yourself the question: Am I doing this for my children's sake or mine? Be sure you are not crossing the line of what is reasonable and that everything you do is in the very, very best interests of your children and is not some tactical manoeuvre with which to score points off your ex (perhaps an understandable thing to want to do in certain circumstances).

If you work closely with your lawyer, you and your ex can achieve the best possible contact plan and relationship with your children.

At first it will feel inconceivable that you should have to apply such definitions to you, your partner and your children – and inconceivable that your once single-entity family will now be a split unit.

In your pre-children days, you and your partner formed a heartland as a couple. You were one another's emotional, physical and spiritual mate. You had to think of no one but each other. Once children came along you transferred your focus and primary energies into your children. Then they took centre stage in the unit – and became the bedrock of a revised heartland.

The changes post-divorce are momentous for all. Your joint task is to split your time fairly, realistically and **meaningfully**. You will have to search for and build upon yet another new heartland – this time a third incarnation of the original unit. Now is the moment to really look at your family's dynamics, bonds and relationships in detail. That includes wider family, close and distant relatives, friends and godparents (see Chapter One, 'Preparing to Divorce').

NAVIGATING THROUGH THE MINEFIELD

Whilst you are facing the demise of your family it is certain that social mores, other people's judgements and emotions will be ricocheting off the walls. You are going to have to pause, draw a very deep breath and be conciliatory and reasonable for the sake of your children in order to maintain and facilitate the most important relationships of your life.

It doesn't take a rocket scientist to work out why the process becomes so much more complex when children are involved. You do not have the luxury of being able to focus on 'you' and your rehabilitation but the upside is that you will not be able to wallow in your divorce – your children's needs make this almost impossible. Tending to their bloodied knees, food intolerances and chemistry homework really can be a blessing in disguise and can be a way to heal and re-focus your energies on a new life.

Pre-divorce, you cannot begin to imagine how gut-wrenching it is and what heartache it will cause. You will need to be formidably strong and as a mother you must be the bigger and better person at all times. There will inevitably be moments when all you will want to do is sit in a heap in the middle of the floor and sob your eyes out from sheer exhaustion (or grief) but it is essential that you at least try to keep these aberrations away from your children. This is not to say that you should bottle up your emotions – it is a veritable skill (that you can learn) to be able to release your sadness and upset through crying – every single day, if possible – but just not in front of your children. They are going through enough on their own and will be deeply distressed to see you in such a state. According to one of our former GPs, stress is considered to be 75 per cent exhaustion – so ensure you get enough sleep and be kind to yourself.

Health Warning: whilst you and your ex are still together and trying to work out a suitable arrangement for the children, all may appear to be amicable. But from the moment you file for divorce this will inexorably change and your children will become part of the mix and the territory of the new battle-ground. It will shock you all and disturb your family equilibrium. You may find that you cannot agree on a single matter and this will inevitably include the children. The involved father can go. This will be a loss to you all.

In nine out of ten cases young children will live with their mother but there is no rule to that effect.

THE RULES

Rule One
Your children should, and must, have a good and solid relationship with *both* parents. That is a prerequisite and is non-negotiable. The law's viewpoint is that your children have the right to see both parents. You and your partner do *not* have a right to see *them*.

Rule Two
Never use your children as a weapon, a shield or in retaliation for something that your ex may have done to hurt *you*.

If he is not paying maintenance for a real or fabricated reason he and the children still *should and must spend time together*.

If he has just introduced a new girlfriend six weeks after your split or has only known her very briefly and has introduced her as their 'new mother' it is not something you can influence or change, however much you might want to. You can certainly rant and rave to yourself. But should you really? Is your own jealousy rearing its green-tressed head? If so, then deal with it. If you have no feelings for your ex-partner and think it may harm your children to see Daddy with a new woman in his life, there is nothing you can do. Harsh but true. You cannot use your emotions on either count as a valid reason to stop your partner seeing his children. The vast majority of men that we interviewed for our Perspectives chapter (Chapter 10) had all experienced the harrowing scenario of their ex-wives attempting to prevent them from seeing their children – as retaliation for a perceived or real event. This is never a wise thing to do, not only because it is simply wrong from a moral perspective but also because it will ultimately damage your children.

Unless there are very solid grounds for preventing your ex from seeing your children (see Chapter 5, 'Extreme Divorce'), you might as well face up to it now – and before you end up spending vast sums of money through the courts. We know many couples who have ended up virtually bankrupting themselves in order to maintain a tug-of-war vendetta against their spouses and also know of children who have ultimately 'voted with their feet' at the earliest opportunity and moved to live *permanently* with the parent that they were originally prevented from seeing. So tread carefully and repress any urges you may feel to take some kind of ill-thought-through revenge on your ex. It isn't worth it.

You may have some verbal agreement that if either of you has a partner you will give the children time to adjust and get to know the other person. For example, you undertake not to 'sleep' with them in the same house whilst the children are around until you have had time to discuss this gently with them. This will all mean nothing. If either one of you has another person in your life – however transitory – you will be feeling and supporting diametrically opposed views.

It will hurt a lot to realize that you no longer have a say in everything that happens in your child's upbringing. But it can help if you think that such feelings come from the 'ego' and are possibly more about your personal pride than about the need for your children to see their father, however imperfect he is and however messy the split.

Rule Three

Never share your opinions about their father with your children. Children will pick up on your mood and your feelings as if by osmosis. They are his children as much as they are yours. Do try to suppress any bad thoughts about their father and refrain from articulating them. Write them down in a diary to offload them if you must and make a contemporaneous note if you think that something is important from a legal perspective.

Children hear and see far more than we imagine. Do you remember how you absorbed atmospheres and emotions from your parents when you were a child without really knowing why? Always be economical with the truth where they are concerned and protect them from any angst and worry that you feel. They will not understand and should not have to deal with what you are carrying, no matter what their age. Equally, don't expect them to share what is happening at Daddy's house with you. It will also help you to move on far quicker if you think of their life with him as completely separate.

Older children will clearly be more involved but protect them wherever possible – you will never regret it.

With younger children use stock phrases, for example:, 'Daddy and Mummy are just being silly', 'Daddy is being tricky right now' or 'Daddy and I need to work some things out – don't worry'. These sound like platitudes and **they are** but you will need them to placate and diffuse any tension for them. You need to be consistent and repetitive.

It does make a difference what ages your children are. Just as you need to gauge the temperature in your relationship with your partner – how up to speed are they with what is going on? How are they reacting? We have been very clear about the way you should try to behave, react and speak to your children. Answer their questions honestly and openly but be measured for their sake. Sometimes it is best to be economical with the truth. Do not allow yourself to be overheard sharing gory details about your partner with a friend, which could be deemed as a criticism of your partner. Your children may feel that they should be taking sides – and it is not fair to put them in such a dilemma. One overheard loose word or derogatory rant can undo all the hard work of not talking badly about your partner face to face with your children.

ALIENATION

It is vitally important to rise above the emotional mayhem and the intensity of your feelings when dealing with contact negotiation. You and your ex must not attempt to influence your children against the other, however tempting. The technical term for this is **alienation**. The desire to overlay your feelings onto your children is plain wrong. It will cause your children so much pain and anguish. They will be going through enough and this will add to their stress levels.

There are instances where mothers and fathers have gone against Rule One and actively tried to manipulate the children's feelings and emotions. They have created and exaggerated scenarios in order to force their children to side with them. A typical example of this is where the father tries to imply that you are a 'bad mother'. This could be a fabricated or exaggerated accusation just for effect, e.g., 'She leaves the children with unqualified nannies, goes travelling all over the world and is hardly ever at home.'

The facts are you have probably been abroad for a

couple of nights on business or to visit a friend or relative. When you hear this cited against you, even though you know the facts are twisted, do not decide to retaliate! Be guided by your lawyer and be confident that he will be able to demonstrate that this is being used as a tactical manoeuvre to damage your contact position and credibility.

It is extremely hard to witness behaviour from your partner that you totally disagree with or believe to be harming your children emotionally and mentally – or, even worse, physically. It is even harder to follow the due process, not least because of the length of time this can take. However, if your ex's behaviour is genuinely affecting your child then attempting to restrict his contact through the courts is something you should consider. It is a serious step and can have far-reaching effects, but if you keep in mind that whatever you do is in the best interests of your child and that is validated via the courts then you can rest assured that you are doing the right thing.

It is always wise to be close by younger children when they are having indirect contact with your ex. Young children can find it hard to grasp the concept of the phone, email or Skype so if you know their father is going to call, give them some subjects to speak about – and prompt them. Some men may think this is eavesdropping, but it is actually facilitating the process of communication and should be encouraged.

All conversations with the children should be capable of being shared or held with the other parent present without any issue. No parent should have a 'private' conversation with their children or manufacture the promise for one. This is divisive and sets up a 'them and us' atmosphere when what you are trying to achieve is a sense of unity – albeit in different locations!

Older children may need encouragement, too. Against a backdrop of loss and anger, teenagers can clam up. Get them to share what they are doing at school or on the football pitch. If emotions are running high and older children do not want to speak, they need to be the ones to tell their father that they do not want to speak or email – not you.

HANGOVER FROM ALCOHOL OR DRUG ABUSE

If you have *ever* had any issues with alcohol or drug abuse then we suggest you are transparent about this and confront the issue up front and without reservation in the divorce process. Similarly, if you have recently lapsed back into alcohol or substance abuse then we suggest you seek immediate help – and tell your lawyer. In this way your lawyer will be prepared and in a position to counteract the tactical use of any evidence by your partner in the appropriate manner.

The following websites can be a first step or consult your family GP:

www.alcoholics-anonymous.org.uk

www.helpguide.org

www.talktofrank.com

THE NEW LAW – APRIL 2014

When we wrote this book the terms 'residence' and 'contact' were used to describe the orders usually made by the courts in children cases. As a result of changes that came into effect on 22 April 2014, these concepts have been combined in the new Child Arrangements Order, which sets out arrangements relating to with whom and when a child is to live, spend time or otherwise have contact with any other person.

The new procedure places greater emphasis on mediation and other forms of 'non-court resolution' of disputes. How much practical difference these changes will make remains to be seen and whatever label is used, it is still helpful to understand what the courts and lawyers mean by these terms because we suspect that they will remain in common usage for the foreseeable future.

LEGAL JARGON

As the mother of your children you have automatic **Parental Responsibility** (PR).

If you and your partner are married, then the children's father will have automatic **Parental Responsibility** (PR). This concept is given increased emphasis under the recent changes.

If you and your partner are not married – but are going through a legal separation there are several options that you need to consider:

- If your child was born before 1 December 2003 and your partner is not named on the birth certificate then you will need to re-register the birth and name their father formally on the birth certificate and amend this to include the father's name.
- You and your partner can make a formal Parental Responsibility Agreement (without changing the birth certificate) by going to the Courts Service website: www.hmcourts-service.gov.uk
- Similarly your partner may look to apply to the court for PR if you have not been supportive of your partner in this respect. Ensure that you take legal advice if this is the sole area you are contesting as finances may be taken into consideration independently.

- If your child was registered after 1 December 2003, then you will need to make a formal Parental Responsibility agreement with their father. In this instance the father will most likely initiate this but either one of you can do this.

Residence (formerly 'custody') is pretty self-explanatory – simply where and with whom the child lives.

Joint or Shared Residence means that the child lives with each parent in two different places for part of the time. It does *not* mean that the time is split equally – a common misconception that causes frequent disputes. It is very common for fathers denied what they feel to be sufficient contact with their child to retaliate by applying for joint residence in the belief that that entitles them to a guaranteed 50 per cent of the child's time. It doesn't: indeed joint residence orders are rarely made in that situation simply because it only really works when the parents can cooperate together, i.e., act jointly, hence 'joint residence'. The very fact that the courts have been involved at all is a pretty clear indication that they can't. A reasonable and cooperative arrangement is unlikely if the parents involved can't even communicate except through lawyers. The better option is residence with Mum or Dad but with very generous contact for the non-resident parent.

Contact (formerly 'access' – never the American 'visitation') is the time that a child spends with another person – usually the non-resident parent though it is also applied to grandparents and other people with whom the child has a relationship.

- Ideally the parents will agree a flexible arrangement, i.e., reasonable contact but if not, contact will be **defined,** i.e., specific times and dates for visits, overnight stays and holidays

will be set out in a court order. It will require you to allow
contact and to be responsible for making the order work.

- It can be **direct** (i.e., physically spending time together) or
  indirect (i.e., phone calls, letters, birthday presents, etc.).
  Direct contact may or may not be staying (i.e., overnight). You
  will most likely be in the position where you are the parent
  with whom your children reside, therefore this relates to
  your partner having contact with your children (afternoons,
  overnight/weekend stays/lunch and holidays).
- Contact may be supervised by a family member or at a contact
  centre, which provides facilities for secure and observed
  contact sessions – but at a cost.

A **Prohibited Steps Order** has the effect of restraining your
partner or family member from doing specific things. *This
can only be made by the court.* Issues that could be contained in this type of order might be a change of surname
from the father's or preventing him from taking a child
out of the country if, for example, he was irresponsible or
incapable. This is a *very serious court measure* and should
be invoked only when a solution cannot be agreed via due
process in the divorce proceedings. In the event of an emergency, A Prohibited Steps Order – or any other Section 8
order – can be applied *without your partner or other party
being notified.* Examples of an emergency might be to allow
(or prevent) medical intervention or to prevent your ex from
attempting to abscond or emigrate with your child.

Specific Issue Order – This type of order relates to a specific question – for example where your child is schooled.

WHAT THE COURT CAN DO – TIME FOR THE TECHNICAL STUFF

The court's powers to make Child Arrangements Orders about contact or residence are contained in the Children Act 1989 (as amended) and its approach is governed by these three basic principles:

1. The welfare of the child, not its parents' wishes, is paramount and the child should be at the centre of all decision making.
2. Delay is likely to prejudice the child's welfare.
3. The court should not make any order unless it considers that doing so would be better for the child than making no order at all.

When deciding what to do, the court *must* have regard to the following factors (known as **the welfare checklist**), which include:

- The wishes and feelings of the child
- His or her physical, emotional and educational needs
- The likely impact of any changes
- The child's age, sex and background
- Any harm he has suffered (or is at risk of suffering)
- How capable each parent is of meeting the child's needs
- The range of powers available to the court under the proceedings.

An important point to note is that the court does not *have* to make any sort of Child Arrangements Order – the best arrangements are flexible and informal so if you and your ex can make an arrangement work between you, all well and good. So long as the judge is satisfied that there is no need for the court to exercise its powers, then the courts will not interfere.

Of equal importance is the point that nowhere in the welfare checklist is there any reference to the 'rights' of the parents. Children are not a possession to be claimed, owned or awarded.

APPLICATIONS TO COURT – THE NEW PROCEDURE

From 22 April 2014, all disputes between separated parents or family about arrangements concerning children are governed by the **Child Arrangements Programme**, which sets out a framework of rules and principles that govern what will happen. It is available online and is essential reading.

There is only space to set out the aims and structure of the programme here. Generally, except in very specific circumstances, the courts will no longer consider any application until the parties have attended a Mediation Information and Assessment Meeting – 'MIAM'.

The application submitted by your solicitor will state the reasons for the application and the type of order you require. An application is normally about two sides of A4 and will be well spaced to allow for amendments. On first receiving a draft copy it may seem like a travesty of all that you and your children are going through and can be very upsetting.

Legal Aid provision is possible to assist with the cost of the MIAM and mediation, but otherwise you will have to pay for this. In addition, you will usually have to pay for your lawyer to process the application to court.

Once made, the application will be allocated by a judge to one of several different levels of Family Court Judge who is likely to hear the case from start to finish.

The court will normally fix a FHDRA (First Hearing Dispute Resolution Appointment – for more details, see Chapter 6, 'Court Process') five weeks later to allow time for CAFCASS (The Children and Family Court Advisory and Support Service) to complete safeguarding checks. CAFCASS officers are social workers of the court and are assigned if the court decides that it needs their involvement to provide a background investigation report. CAFCASS will typically interview you, your children and your ex-partner. They will carry out background police and social services checks to see if the parents or the children have been the subject of police or children's services involvement. (Please note CAFCASS operates only in England; www.cafcass. gov.uk.)

At the FHDRA hearing the judge will give orders (directions) to take the case forward but the main aim is to see whether the case is suitable for 'non-court resolution' through the help of CAFCASS, sending the parties on a Separated Parents Information Programme or further mediation.

The new framework places great emphasis on the importance of the child knowing that his or her wishes and feelings are being considered. Reports may be ordered from CAFCASS or the local authority to help the court find out more about the background or the children's wishes and feelings. If no agreement can be reached, the court will next fix a Dispute Resolution Appointment for when the Report will be to hand – probably at least eight weeks later. In cases where there are disputed allegations of domestic violence or abuse that have to be established or disproved before a final decision can be made, the court may order a fact-finding hearing.

Ultimately, if the dispute remains intractable, there will

be a final hearing at which both parties will give evidence and the judge will decide the outcome.

Your diligent approach to making contemporaneous notes and being clear in what you are trying to achieve through the order is of paramount importance now and will help the application process enormously. Be focused in what you are applying for and ensure that your lawyer is aware of all the facts.

You are likely to have many questions about all this. How can a judge possibly gauge my situation? How dire is this problem for my family? Be strong and if you have been clear and you trust your lawyer then you will know that he will be aware of the background. Perhaps you also need to believe that they have seen similar and worse before and your lawyer will fill in the gaps for the judge in court in any event. A legal 'bundle' will normally be given to the judge that will contain detailed information about your case. It is very easy to worry ceaselessly that the judge 'doesn't get it' or that he may not 'see through' your ex. Don't worry and trust in the process.

If you are appearing in court alongside your lawyer, be sure to have a short meeting beforehand. Your lawyers will then have the opportunity to explain how the hearing will proceed and what he will be expecting the judge to focus on.

You may wonder how thirty minutes can possibly be sufficient for a hearing, especially when you have seen the two sides of A4, but it will be enough. Use this time with your lawyer(s) to calm your nerves as you will undoubtedly be feeling apprehensive, vulnerable or even traumatized. This is normal! However confident you may feel before the hearing, at the actual moment you will realize just how vitally important it is to your future with your children. It will be a hugely emotional event.

Be kind to yourself and enlist the support of your real friends (see Chapter One, 'Preparing to Divorce'). They will not be allowed into the courtroom with you but can be with you in the waiting room before and after the hearing and when you are with your lawyer. If you are going to court by car make sure that you ask a friend to drive you there. You don't need the extra anxiety of worrying about how to get to court or whether you will find a parking space. This is the time to lean on those closest to you.

Where the attitude of the children to contact or residence is concerned, a **Wishes and Feelings Report** will be ordered that highlights the feelings/concerns and desires of the child – not you. The report can be done with any child old enough to articulate their feelings – and a good CAFCASS officer will have a variety of ways of ascertaining these from younger children. However, the older the child, the greater weight will usually be attached by the court to their wishes. The contents are then shared with you, your lawyer, your ex and the court.

WHAT THE CHILDREN WANT

Even young children will have opinions and feelings about how – and when – they should see their parents, but cannot necessarily articulate them. You and your partner need to respect these wholeheartedly, irrespective of what is going on in your relationship. The problem is that most warring parents don't.

Things that are happening in their parents' lives colour the way children feel and these can change day by day or as quickly as from one moment to the next. Be alert to their mood changes and watch out for fundamental changes in their behaviour, which could signal a need to seek professional help, e.g. if a child becomes very withdrawn (Chapter Two, 'Preparing Your Child for Separation').

You need to work out if there is a real reason for your child wanting to change the structure of the contact regime. Could it be a cry for help? The pattern of emotion is critical in this instance. During the divorce process children may want to increase their contact, reduce it or stop it altogether with *either one of you* and you need to be prepared and brutally honest with yourself as to why this might be.

Contact is a bit like a patchwork quilt of your family's new life. The piecing together of the quilt needs to include events, memories and a firm structure in order to produce a harmonious and comfortable blanket for the future of your children. From this place the children can feel safe to express themselves, see and love both parents freely and equally.

You have to be very bold, honest and authentic with yourself. You must be totally grounded when it comes to contact plans. Nor must you be spiteful or vindictive towards your partner as this will completely backfire.

ROTTEN EGG

If you are dealing with a man who is only interested in contact with his children in order to play games with *you*, this can be enormously disruptive to your new family unit. Perhaps the father is unhappy, insecure, delusional, controlling, selfish – or just not a good egg! If this is the case, you will need to build up a storyboard of his behaviour and examples that support this view. These elements will need to be factual and robust.

PATERNAL MYOPIA

What happens if one or both of your children do not want to see their father at all? Typically this might happen with older children but can happen from the age of eight or nine – or even earlier. The age and strength of a child's feelings must be genuinely sustained over time. You cannot rely on a one-off instance where your child comes back from a weekend and says, 'Daddy was cross with me because I broke a lamp – I never want to see him again.' This is clearly just a child's reaction to being told off.

STEP-PARENTS

Step-parents are not automatically entitled to the same rights and responsibilities as biological parents. No matter how close the bond might be between the step-parent and the child, parental responsibility can only be achieved by making a formal agreement between step-parents and the child's biological parents. Alternatively, contact can be achieved through a court order.

For more information visit: www.childcustodylawyer. co.uk/services

DIRECT CONTACT

When it comes to setting an arrangement in place for Direct Contact there are a few things you will need to think about. It will be hard not to feel jealous and lonely when your children are not with you in the early stages of your separation. Be aware that a previously quite absent father can have regarded himself as simply fulfilling his role as a father/breadwinner by prioritizing work. This does not mean in any way that the father doesn't love his children and want to spend time with them. It just means he's not very good at it. The prospect of sudden separation from his children (however little he may have seen them before) is likely to make him feel threatened. If the father genuinely wants to keep and maintain regular and supportive direct contact, this is great – so encourage it.

If not, he will likely feel he has to go on the attack – making demands without really considering what contact the children want or need, what he wants and can sustain, and how that will actually work (see joint residence below). Men often (wrongly) see the process as a contest that they will win or lose. They think (wrongly) that throwing mud will help their case. He may well interpret any attempts by his lawyer to suggest a compromise as weakness on his part. It's vital that both parties understand what the court's approach and ultimate aim is.

In the rare situation where his behaviour is both tactical and disruptive, it is possible that your partner has decided that he wants to 'take the children away from you'. Unless there is some compelling reason, he is highly unlikely to succeed. At best this is difficult and upsetting – and at worst terrifying and traumatic. Men know that the way to a woman's heart is through her children and your ex might very well use the children to frustrate, undermine and even destroy you.

In the event that you have managed a mutually agreed and mutually upheld contact plan, we would hope that if changes were needed you would be able to discuss these sensibly and even involve the children if necessary.

A contact plan should have routine and at the beginning – when everything is in a state of flux – established dates and times. This makes it very clear to both sides what and when things will happen. Draw up a table and treat it like a work commitment.

KEY PRINCIPLES FOR CONTACT

- **C**onsistent – Not all contact periods need to be the same but it's no good having a day's contact one weekend then thirty minutes the next. Agree when and for how long and stick to it.
- **P**redictable – If you agree to contact every other weekend plus one or two nights in the intervening week (a common pattern) then stick to it. Don't try to change the pattern except for special occasions – but agree the changes well in advance, not as you hand them over the week before. This is particularly true of Christmas and school holidays.
- **R**eliable – Both you and your ex must keep religiously to times and dates. This is one of the biggest causes of disputes. Be on time.

If you have an interim arrangement with your ex during the divorce process, this can be changed by mutual consent and there is no need to accept something that is not working for ever. Don't change things unilaterally because that destroys trust, gives your ex the idea that you are dictating to him and tends to spark a dispute.

Establish holiday dates early on – and a year in advance if possible so that you both know exactly where you stand. Remember that communication is likely to deteriorate so it is best to do this now. It is important to take into account your child's commitments – school trips or music exams, for example.

It is quite typical for children in the UK to see their father every other weekend from school pick-up on Friday or on a Saturday morning from home. Drop-off can be Sunday night or on a Monday morning back at school. Some judges favour a Sunday-night return to ensure readiness for school for purely practical reasons.

TELL THAT *!X.,*! $*! *'$*!*&! TO ...
Don't use your children as messengers. Have a notebook in which you and he can write down anything that needs saying and send to and fro between the two homes. This has a number of advantages:

- It keeps the children out of the fray.
- It avoids confusion.
- It provides you with a record of what was said.

Health Warning: if your children have to take overnight bags to school this can cause them to feel 'different' and can make their situation even more obvious to other children. If practical, consider picking them up from school as normal and then have them collected by their father from home.

Some fathers like to have, and can manage mid-week contact. This can take the form of a supper out or an overnight stay. It's always going to be disruptive. That's not a reason not to do it. Children still have to do homework, football practice or orchestra or whatever. Dad has to accept that. Children can accommodate almost anything as long as it is CPR (Consistent, Predictable, Reliable).

When they go to their father it can be 'fun' – supper out, a movie and playing with the new Xbox that Daddy bought to make his home more appealing. These things are absolutely great to make the children feel welcome and at home and also provide them with things to do. Encourage all these things with your child.

Sometimes you need to speak on behalf of your children despite the inevitable waves this will create. It is virtually certain that if you suggest that some contact is not in the best interests of the children that you will be accused of wanting to restrict the contact. You must have real and valid reasons for any change in the contact arrangements and trying to offer alternatives is a reasonable thing to do.

Watch out for your child's belongings and clothes not being returned from your ex's house. It can be exasperating and you will need extra time and energy to sort out the hassle of such 'trivial' matters. But such things happen when people are being derailed by divorce and your ex may wish to create as much disruption and hurt to you as possible.

It should all be about giving your child the best quality contact at the right times and with all the comfort and security they need in a very difficult transitional period in their lives. You must support your children in accepting your partner's new life but if his hobbies are impacting on their time with him they will soon not want to spend time with him. They will see that they are there because they 'have to be' and they may not say anything for a long time so as to not offend or upset either party. Men are typically not used to the demands of childcare. Having said that, we know loads of men who are impeccable role-models of fatherhood and cannot be faulted! It is all down to the individual situation.

It is hard to create a world with two actual homes. Your children will have a home and whilst it is nice to think of having two homes this is not really the case. Whichever house your children live in most of the time will be their home. It is important that this is the case for their sake – to have a single place of security and stability. Obviously it is important that your ex makes an effort to create the right child-friendly environment with familiar toys, games and duvet covers from home – and you can help with this.

FIGHTING IT OUT – THE OK CORRAL

You might find yourself fighting over the return of a pink teddy bear or the really special clothes you sent over for the weekend. You might find that you are asked to provide and buy things to support your ex's contact while the children are with him. Again it is important to PAUSE and see if this is a pattern of behaviour to frustrate and exasperate you. If it is then you will need to rise above it, fight for Mr Pink Bear or let it go for now – but make a note of it as an example of how he is using the contact negotiation and the contact itself as a tool.

A good starting point is to ask your ex to buy some clothes so some are always at his home instead of carting bags of stuff back and forth. Recognize that this may not be possible. Perhaps he refuses because he considers that he pays maintenance and it should be your expenditure or perhaps he just wishes to burden you with the packing and unpacking. If you are receiving child maintenance then typically it will be your responsibility.

If your ex likes to make things difficult for you, then the logistics and organization of contact is a good platform for him to do this. He may religiously check the contents of the bags once he arrives at his home with the children. If anything is missing he might text or email you accusing you of 'doing it on purpose' and 'trying to ruin his time with the children' as they didn't have their favourite jumper. We have heard of extreme cases where the father has decided to deduct the cost of a simple toothbrush from the next month's maintenance payment.

INTERNATIONAL ASPECTS

All jurisdictions are different and seeking expert local advice is essential. Many countries recognize and will enforce each other's court orders.

Wherever you are in the world, you will need to make a robust contact order.

There are three possible scenarios:

1. You have both decided to stay overseas
2. You want to return to the UK with your children
3. You wish to stay overseas and your partner wishes to return to the UK

If you are abroad, unless you have agreed with your partner that you can relocate to another legal jurisdiction, you *may* need to divorce in the country where you are currently residing with the children, even if you are a non-resident. This is extremely important to remember! We know of women who have been trapped in a country for several years, not being able to leave with their children until the divorce was final.

The initial constraints may be that you cannot leave your current country of residence or expat residence and will need your partner's permission to leave with the children – unless, of course, he doesn't care. In reality this means you will need permission to visit friends and family with your children if that means going abroad. In some instances you may be forced to evidence your whereabouts even if you travel somewhere overnight if your partner thinks you may abscond with the children. This may seem ridiculous, especially if you have given a legal undertaking not to leave the country without permission – but it is the norm in some countries or just because your ex wants control.

As we live in a global village be sure to include all travel scenarios whilst you are divorcing (not necessary in the UK) so there are detailed parameters and there can be no confusion. List friends and family and formally request the option that you can go on holiday with your children on your own at home and abroad – if you inform him of dates and telephone numbers. If your partner is stipulating such constraints on you, ensure that you have reciprocal restrictions for him.

We are not able to cover all countries' legal process in this book, but our guidance is that you take legal advice and if you are in a similar situation ensure you have a lawyer. Seek their advice and construct a contact and travel/visit order that gives you and your children the freedom to lead a life whilst going through your divorce process.

CHAPTER NINE

Post-divorce Management

*'You can never cross the ocean until you have the courage to lose
sight of the shore...'*

Christopher Columbus

LIFE AFTER DECREE ABSOLUTE

This chapter covers everything you will need to know after
your divorce is finalized, e.g., professional negligence, resort
to the Legal Ombudsman, management of maintenance
and contact issues, resort to CMS (Child Maintenance
Service previously known as the Child Support Agency),
non-compliance and enforcement of orders and transfer of
property and other assets.

CHOCS AWAY!

Congratulations! You are now in possession of your Decree
Absolute – and you should consider it your passport to a
brand-spanking-new future for you and your children.

It is entirely understandable that you might feel like
collapsing into an exhausted and anti-climactic heap at this
point but it is absolutely essential that you avoid doing this,
if at all possible. It may at times have seemed like a gruelling
(and never-ending!) ordeal so when you are holding this
rather unremarkable piece of paper in your hand at the end
of it all, it may feel mildly disappointing – even a bit of a

let-down. This applies even when you could not be more overjoyed at the fact that you and your former husband are now two distinctly separate units. The process is so intense and long-winded that your initial euphoria may long ago have been replaced by a type of mild apathy.

You almost certainly have a few grey hairs and wrinkles to show for all your tribulations, and the unrelenting levels of stress are bound to have taken their toll upon you. Anyone who professes to emerge from divorce completely unscathed is either lying or profoundly delusional! So it will probably come as a bit of a shock to learn that the process is not quite finished and that there are a number of loose ends that you will need to tie up.

SALUT LA VIE EN ROSE

This is not the time to let your guard slip or to take your finger off the pulse but it *is* the time to celebrate! Like all rites of passage it is vital from a psychological perspective to acknowledge this memorable goal you have reached and to give yourself a very large slap on the back. Since the dawn of time, man (and woman!) has been holding rituals and ceremonies to mark the transition from one period of life to another (birth, coming of age, marriage, etc.), and divorce is no less important, just because it is a private and intensely personal event – and because card manufacturers don't make their profits from divorce party invitations.

According to the early twentieth-century anthropologist Arnold van Gennep (whose theories are still more relevant today than ever), there is a three-phase structure to a rite of passage:

- Separation
- Transition
- Aggregation

In other words, a person has to be fully separated from – and 'moved-on' from – one role before he or she can be fully 'incorporated' into a new one. Rituals and ceremonies facilitate this transition and they give a very real and tangible structure to something that could otherwise be perceived as quite 'abstract', fleeting and fragile.

If you do not feel like throwing a party – or even going for a drink with a few close friends (and we can entirely understand why you would *not* feel like doing this; you might just prefer to have a long bath and an early night) – then it is worth marking the event privately. There are an infinite number of ways you could choose to do this but they could include: burying your wedding ring in a secret place in your garden, selling your rings and using the money to take you and your children on a much-needed holiday, having your engagement ring recrafted into another item of jewellery such as a brooch or earrings or burning some old photos or divorce documents that caused you pain (not the Decree Absolute!) and then scattering or burying the ashes. Anything that draws a line and marks the event with a ceremonial gesture, however small, will help to attest to the fact *for you* that the marriage really is finally over and that a new era is beginning.

DISPUTES – JUST WHEN YOU THOUGHT IT WAS SAFE...

WHAT TO DO WHEN YOU ARE IN DISPUTE WITH YOUR SOLICITOR

If you are having problems or unresolved issues with your solicitor it is likely that you will have been aware of these *before* your divorce was finalized – but this is not always the case.

Disputed Bill

You may suddenly be presented with a bill that was substantially more than you were originally quoted. If this is the case, your first port of call should *always* be the firm of solicitors that acted for you and if you are not able to resolve your query with the individual solicitor who has been handling your case then you should make a formal complaint in writing to the Senior Partner of the firm. In the normal course of things this is usually sufficient and in the case of a disputed bill the firm will usually seek to resolve the matter by discounting the bill – especially if it is not what was agreed – and even more so, if the amount has added up with no warning and no interim fee notes have been sent to you.

The Legal Ombudsman

If the firm is unwilling to discount your bill then you can contact the Legal Ombudsman by visiting its website at: www.legalombudsman.org.uk.

You will very quickly be assigned a representative who will attempt to act as a mediator between the two parties.

You will be required to fill in a form that outlines the grounds for your complaint and the reasons why you think the bill is too high. The Legal Ombudsman normally acknowledges your complaint very quickly and always aims to settle a dispute as promptly as possible – usually within a couple of months. However, there is no guarantee that it is always as impartial a body as you might hope and it is quite possible that you will find yourself still expected to pay more than you feel is fair or warranted. If you think that you have substantial grounds for persisting with your complaint then you should appeal. You can do this by going over the head of the officer you have been dealing with and appealing to his or her manager. It is *always* best to inform the person you have been dealing with that you are not satisfied with their decision (which is actually only a recommendation) and that you are proposing to do this.

Professional Negligence

If the dispute is not to do with the amount of the bill but relates to some step or process that your solicitor failed to implement then it is important to make your complaint formally – in writing – and as quickly as possible from the time you discover the anomaly. An example of this might be that you discover that your solicitor did not take sufficient steps to ensure your financial security, for instance they may not have protected your rights by securing a charge over a property that might become vulnerable to other creditors; perhaps your ex sold a property without your knowledge or permission and part or all of your divorce settlement was paid out to other creditors who *did* have a charge over the property; perhaps your solicitor miscalculated the division of assets or your partner's income; perhaps you have not yet paid the bill and are withholding payment until the matter is sorted.

Whatever the situation, if there is a 'stalemate' and the firm is not prepared to put the situation right – *or are suing you* for unpaid fees that you feel are not payable – then it is important that you take independent legal advice as a matter of urgency because there is usually a deadline for complaints.

Please be aware that in order to prove Professional Negligence you need to be able to prove that the losses you have sustained have been brought about as a *direct result* of the actions or non-actions of your lawyer. If you have run out of funds (and we can understand why that might be the case!) you can ask another firm if they will act for you on a no-win, no-fee basis. This means that in the event that they do not win your case for you, you will not be liable for their fees in the claim. If a firm does not consider your claim sufficiently water-tight, it may be difficult for you to find a firm that will act for you but **persevere!** If you have solid grounds to believe in the validity of your case then eventually you are likely to find a firm that will be prepared to act for you (even if it is not on a no-win, no-fee basis) – and a firm that will wait for its fees.

A last resort is to the Legal Ombudsman (as before) or you can represent your claim yourself (see the Health Warning about this at the beginning of Chapter Three, 'How to File for Divorce'). Be aware also that if you are seeking compensation for professional negligence, the Legal Ombudsman rarely awards compensation worth more than a few hundred pounds – or a few thousand pounds in really exceptional cases – so if you can get a lawyer to lodge a defence and counterclaim on your behalf that is without doubt the best route to follow. The Legal Ombudsman will not act for you if you are receiving legal advice elsewhere – so be careful! If you lodge a complaint with the Legal Ombudsman you cannot sue a firm through a separate route at the same time. If large sums of money are involved it is very important to remember this. Do not be prepared to accept a small amount in compensation awarded by the Legal Ombudsman if you know that you are owed a great deal more money by the firm. You can, however, suspend your claim with the Legal Ombudsman in order to preserve any potential claim with them.

AWKWARD SQUAD BEHAVIOUR FROM YOUR EX

Just because you are now a divorcee, it does not mean that overnight your brave new world will be completely trouble-free when it comes to your ex-husband. If he has made it his life's work to make your life gruesome before and during the divorce process it is likely that he will continue to try to make life just as miserable for you post Decree Absolute. The most effective way for him to do this is to obstruct, deny or simply ignore the orders that have been put in place by the courts – be they to do with contact, maintenance, the payment of school fees, or even selling a property to pay for the divorce settlement.

Neither the court nor your solicitor will keep your file for ever – both will destroy them after a number of years – so make sure you get and keep copies now of all court orders made, particularly the Decree Nisi and Decree Absolute, the final financial order and anything relating to children. This is particularly important if the court orders record facts that may come into dispute later on (such as violence or abuse) and that have been proved or admitted. You should also try to keep a copy of any statements and CAFCASS welfare reports. Strictly speaking, you are entitled to most of your solicitor's file, although they may ask you to pay for a copy to be taken.

A NEW RELIGION

Even in the rare event that your divorce has been relatively trauma-free and your ex has made every effort to make the transition as comfortable as possible for both of you – it is vital to keep your eye on the ball and supervise what is – *or is not*! – going on. It is no good jumping up and down with frustration if you discover that he has not been keeping up with his maintenance payments three months down the line. You need to be alert to the possibility that he may renege on some or even all of his undertakings – if he is able to get away with it. It is even likely that if *you* are the one who has filed for divorce that obstructing the process will be a particularly enjoyable form of revenge for him – or even a new religion – and he will take great pleasure in drawing out and sabotaging the process every step of the way.

It can feel really chilling to realize that, despite your divorce, your life is still inextricably linked with that of your ex-husband – especially if you have children together – and that he can still wield an enormous element of control over you simply by being stubborn, obstreperous or, ironically, just totally passive. There really is a reason that your marriage vows contain the words 'until death us do part' – and, at times, it can feel like a life sentence.

Let us explore ways in which he can make your life difficult – and steps you can take to counteract such behaviour.

WISH YOU WERE HERE, HA HA...

If the divorce order includes an order that he will pay maintenance (formally known as 'periodical payments') to you and/or an agreement to pay for the children, he may start by paying it and then simply stop. He may even resign from his job because he is determined that you should not receive any money – even though it will dramatically affect him too. If this should happen, it is worth trying to sort the situation out first before contacting your solicitor as it is clearly much cheaper! But make sure you communicate in writing – or confirm what you have agreed verbally so that there is evidence later if needed.

Some ex-husbands delight in behaving in such a way that you are obliged to liaise through solicitors. They know that this will cost you a great deal of money – so do think through, early on, whether or not you can afford to communicate via lawyers post Decree Absolute.

Other husbands suddenly discover the pot of gold at the end of the rainbow (which you always knew was there but forensic accountants were a little out of your league), and you will see him in a shiny new car and swanning off to Thailand or Cuba for some R&R just as soon as the ink has dried on the order. Should you be unable to negotiate directly with your ex because he is elusive or just down-right abusive then do not wait – contact your solicitor who will take legal steps to enforce the moneys owed to you. It's important not to let the arrears build up too much before doing anything: two or three months at most.

Your ex will then usually be liable for any court costs in addition to the debt he owes you. Be aware that this is a process you may have to repeat many times. It can be an exhausting roller coaster but it is worth it to ensure he pays you and your children what the court has ruled he owes.

CHILD MAINTENANCE

CHILD SUPPORT AGENCY (CSA) / CHILD MAINTENANCE SERVICE (CMS)

The CSA was established in 1993 to calculate, collect, enforce and transfer moneys from the non-resident parent to the parent who has day-to-day responsibility and care for a child. In the normal course of things (but not always), it is the mother who is deemed to be the main carer so the CSA will normally calculate an amount that your partner should pay according to his income and where he lives, etc. From November 2013, the CSA stopped taking on new cases but still handles the maintenance of existing cases. The Child Maintenance Service (CMS) has taken over the role that the CSA fulfilled. You can find out more about its ethos and powers by visiting its website at: www.gov.uk/child-maintenance.

The good news is that there are stringent measures the CMS can take to ensure that the father of your child pays what he owes. The less encouraging news is that according to Wikipedia, the CSA had arrears of just under £3.8 billion in 2011 and before 2005 it took an average of 287 days before a case was processed and cleared. Don't therefore expect an instant result – and **don't delay!** If your ex is not paying what he should, then address the situation promptly. We know how easy it can be to put your head in the sand and hope that the issue will go away. It won't – and the longer you wait to put the process in motion, the longer it will take to get the money you are owed.

New legislation brought in by the Government in 2012 means that the CMS now has a range of powers that the CSA did not have before. For example, it can deduct moneys directly from a partner's earnings, take money directly out of his bank or building society account, obtain a liability order through the courts and even send in bailiffs to seize cars, furniture or other assets. Other measures include the non-resident parent being forced to pay for their own legal costs and the costs of the CMS in addition to the arrears in child maintenance.

In really extreme cases, ex-partners can be forced to sell their home or other assets, risk losing their driving licence and even end up facing up to two years in prison. These are probably sufficiently draconian measures to deter even the most 'die-hard' adversary – but you want to ensure that he is paying his share long before this kind of action is necessary.

THE BOTTOMLESS PIT

In a 'typical' divorce where both parents are working, the order may specify that any school fees are jointly and severally payable by the parents. This means that should one parent not be in a position – or refuse – to pay the school fees then the other is legally obliged to pay them. If your ex is particularly vindictive and is more interested in hurting you and disrupting your life than he is in securing a stable education for his children, there is very little you can do about it if he decides to stop paying the school fees – and it can be devastating. One way around this is to arrange a meeting with the school bursar who, if he is at all interested in the child's welfare, may be able to organize a bursary. This may help in the short term or at least until alternative arrangements can be made for your child's schooling. Even taking fee-paying schools out of the equation, children are incredibly expensive to maintain and they get no cheaper the older they get – quite the reverse.

Playing Hooky – Taking Your Child Out of School

Taking your child out of a fee-paying school can be a traumatic event for both parent and child, but it is worth remembering that it can sometimes be more harrowing for the parent. You might be surprised to hear how many people we know who have struggled and made gruelling sacrifices for years to keep their children at schools they could not afford on their own – and went into shocking amounts of debt in order to do this. It was only when they had no alternative but to take their child away and enrol them into a local state school that the child was noticeably – and often instantly – happier. Sometimes the financial struggle can be too much of a burden for the parent – and the child will intuitively absorb the parent's anxiety – and the subsequent and corresponding relief.

WHAT TIME DO YOU CALL THIS?

One way that your ex can make life extremely inconvenient for you is to be unreliable with contact – particularly with regard to holidays. Examples of this are him making your children miss an agreed flight back from their holiday with *him* so that they miss a connection and *you* miss your holiday with them as a result; him not responding to texts or emails so that you are anxious and flustered because you don't know their whereabouts when he has them for a holiday, and him not picking the children up when he says that he will (and does not even contact you to tell you) so that you are forced to change *your* plans or find someone who will look after your children at short notice – and at vast expense. His constant unreliability is key here – see Chapter Eight, 'Contact and Residence' and the importance of keeping diary notes. Please note that we have not repeated all the elements that can arise post your divorce regarding contact because we have covered it in detail in Chapter Eight. Please refer to this again in your post-divorce environment.)

ENFORCEMENT OF AN ORDER – WHAT TO DO WHEN HE WON'T PLAY BALL

In really extreme cases your ex may just refuse to implement measures that the court has ordered such as selling a property to pay for your divorce settlement. There are many ways that he can sabotage a sale, for example: he can put the property on the market with a firm of estate agents and then simply take it off the market again a few days later; he can ensure that the property looks 'unkempt', messy or dirty for viewings, or even make it as difficult as possible for interested parties to view the property at all – by saying viewings have to be during the day/not at weekends, etc.

Be aware that if someone wants to sabotage a sale sufficiently strongly, there is very little you can do about it. Make sure that you are aware of who the agents are and do not be intimidated by your ex. Contact the agents and make sure that you are aware of the situation and developments. Insist that they keep you informed of progress and that they only accept instructions in writing from you both. If they refuse, apply for an order to that effect from the court.

We know of divorces where exes have got a third party to act as a 'stooge' to put in a higher offer for a property when it looked as though a perfectly good offer was about to be accepted. Then the 'stooge' offer was suddenly withdrawn just as soon as the original purchaser had disappeared. The message here is that if someone is going to be awkward they will be – and there is very little that you can do yourself to improve the situation.

In really extreme cases, the only resort you have is to enforce the sale through a lawyer. They can obtain a court order to repossess a property so that the sale is effectively in your hands. Powers include being able to break into a property, evicting your ex and changing the locks and authorizing a third party (usually a District Judge) to sign documents so that they can manage the sale without delay.

These are very extreme and rare situations and we are not suggesting that your divorce will be like this. But it is important to be aware of just how acrimonious divorce can get and that recourse to the courts in situations such as these is the only sensible solution. Bear in mind that your ex will usually be forced to bear the costs of bringing such actions to court plus interest where there has been a delay in the payment of your divorce settlement so long as your lawyers have done their job properly and have provided for this in your divorce order.

TRANSFER OF PROPERTY AND OTHER ASSETS

In a situation where multiple properties are being split at the point of the final divorce order there will be a necessity for that order to be enforced. For example, if there were five properties they would likely be divided 50:50 (though equality is only a starting point – take advice!) and the estimated equity would be calculated across the five properties and the property assets divided based on the equity split. This means that post your divorce there will be enforceable action that you and your ex need to take in a timely fashion, details of which will usually be detailed in the order.

If you are dealing with an individual who decides that he has no interest in signing over the properties to be carried forward in your name, he can prevaricate and obstruct the process for a very long time. One individual we know chose to stop the transfer of properties for two years during which time his ex-wife had to employ lawyers at vast expense via the High Court to force him to sign the paperwork to transfer the properties into her name. Twenty-four hours before the court date he signed the paperwork. The court case still took place as she was adamant that even though he had declared he would sign in writing, he would most probably renege on his undertaking the day after the court case.

To put this in context, the two-year period where she was responsible for the mortgages were during the 2009 crash and the mortgage on the marital home that she desperately needed to sell doubled. Ironically, the judge decided even though she had applied to the court, her ex should not be forced to pay the costs in full – because she would accrue equity on the transfer of the property.

AND NOW FOR THE FUN BIT!

When your divorce is finalized and you have your post-divorce management structure in place, it is then time to turn your attention towards rebuilding your life...

CHAPTER TEN

Perspectives

'Everything we hear is an opinion, not a fact. Everything we see is a perspective, not the truth…'

Marcus Aurelius

Although *A Woman's Guide to Divorce* is indisputably written from a woman's perspective, we wanted to ensure that it retained a very real balance and was not unduly biased in favour of women. In order to do this we interviewed dozens of individuals in the hope of being able to provide an in-depth overview of other people's experiences – and as a result we have come up with a gallery of short 'vignettes' from very different viewpoints.

Here is just a small sample of stories about separation and divorce: from a man's perspective; from an older, retired woman's perspective; from the perspective of young women whose parents divorced when they were teenagers; from the perspective of someone who was a victim of domestic abuse in the days when it was *never* spoken about, and from a judge's and a family solicitor's perspectives. Our interviewees cross the age spectrum – from as young as twenty-one to as old as seventy-five – and they come from all walks of life.

CROSSING THE RUBICON

Despite the extraordinary array of backgrounds, causes and outcomes we came across and the fact that each case is clearly unique, it quickly became obvious to us that it is never one thing that causes a marriage to break down. It is often a series of seemingly unrelated events that contribute to the final collapse of the union and surprisingly frequently it turns out to be something relatively innocuous that is the 'final straw'. It seems that marriage has a breaking point, a 'point of no-return' and *everyone* we interviewed was able to pinpoint the moment when they came to the realization that divorce could be 'on the cards' – and then the 'light bulb' moment at which divorce became inevitable. As the old sentiment goes: if there is a moment when you can see the end, you are already halfway there.

We are simply portraying the facts as they have been presented to us and are not in any way making a judgement call as to the rights and wrongs of the relationships that we have chosen to include. The aim is to provide examples of real-life divorces so that you can perhaps more easily put your own circumstances into perspective…

All names, locations and some details have been changed in order to preserve the anonymity of the individuals concerned.

FROM A MAN'S PERSPECTIVE

GEORGE

Background

George is in his mid-forties, is divorced with two young children and lives with his new girlfriend in Oxfordshire. His ex has the children for most of the time and he now sees them every other weekend and during the holidays. This has not always been the case and in the early days post-separation, his ex-wife prevented him from seeing his children at all. George had to fight through the courts for two years before he was finally granted reasonable contact but prior to this his ex-wife did everything she could to make this impossible.

When George reached his late thirties and realized that all his friends were already married and starting families, he got together with a long-standing friend who was a part of his social circle as both of them had been single for some time. They were both afraid of being on their own (although this was an unspoken understanding) and George admits that peer pressure undoubtedly played a substantial part in his deciding to propose. Four months before the wedding he experienced a severe bout of cold feet but decided to go through with it anyway because of the pressure he was receiving from friends and family.

His ex-wife was very materialistic and everything became about their 'image' – what cars they were driving and what house they were living in. As George is the complete antithesis of pretentious, he found this difficult and it drove an enormous wedge between them. According to George she was a 'narcissist', (his own term) and very controlling of him. As she was by then in her forties, she persuaded him to have children, which according to George was achieved through artificial intervention – so passionless was the marriage. Their relationship finally completely 'fizzled out' and George was forced to walk out of the marriage when their children were three and four years old – he was so intensely miserable in the relationship that he simply could not bear it any longer.

George has always suffered from a very rare condition that was not diagnosed until he was an adult – the two halves of his brain are not connected in a few of the ways that would be considered normal (although you would never guess this if he had not explained this to us). He apparently finds it difficult to pick up on certain social clues that most people would find second nature but it in no way prevents him from being an incredibly intelligent, charming person with a wonderfully engaging, sensitive and gentle personality. His ex-wife used his 'condition' in the divorce proceedings as a reason to prevent him from seeing his children.

Some considerable time later, George found love again after he bumped into a former friend after some twenty years. There had always been a 'spark' but they had been in relationships when they knew each other, so nothing had ever happened between them. By then George was suffering from severe depression, finding it difficult to get out of bed in the mornings and to function normally. He desperately missed his children and could not bear to be separated from them.

George's 'On the Cards' Realization
Before the wedding! He thought that was all there was to life and he might as well resign himself to the reality...

George's 'Light Bulb' Moment

He couldn't bear the 'cold war' of never speaking, the lack of communication – and the total lack of affection.

George's Advice

1. Don't get married just because all your friends are doing it and you think you are on the shelf! Wait for the thunder bolt to strike you. It strikes at different times for different people.
2. Listen to your gut – and not to anyone else! You are the only person that knows what you think and how you feel. Friends mean well but can be completely 'off' when it comes to *your* life and your circumstances.

BEN

Background

Ben met his wife through friends on a large group holiday in Mauritius. Their courtship was very quick and they were married within a year and started a family within two years. Their marriage lasted sixteen years and according to Ben it was ultimately a series of unconnected events that contributed to the breakdown of the marriage. Following all three pregnancies his wife suffered severe post-natal depression, which was compounded by an underlying, chronic thyroid condition that went undiagnosed for years. It made her put on a great deal of weight, obliterated her energy levels and contributed towards her feeling increasingly lethargic and unattractive. This, compounded by lack of sleep with three young boys, meant that the physical side of their relationship was severely affected and the almost total lack of emotional intimacy contributed to a general breakdown in communication and was the precursor to the ultimate divorce.

Major factors that also contributed to the divorce included bereavement (her father died) and the resulting weekly trips for her to visit her mother two hundred miles away. This, although entirely understandable, added to Ben's sense of isolation and the massive cost of the petrol for the weekly round trips alone added to their already deteriorating financial situation. Ben had been made redundant and was unemployed for several months before finding a new, much better paid role – but one that meant that he needed to work long hours and be regularly away on business abroad.

Eventually, he was offered a post in Dubai and although his wife and three small children followed him out and lived with him for the first few months, his wife quickly returned with the children to pursue her own career when a new role came up back in the UK. Ben ended up living on his own in a serviced apartment in Dubai for more than six months and felt increasingly rejected, neglected and isolated. When he returned to the UK, communication with his wife was almost totally non-existent and when his mother-in-law started to interfere in his relationship and accuse him of all sorts of misdemeanours it was the final straw and he confesses that he totally 'lost the plot'.

Ben is now separated and will soon receive his Decree Absolute. His ex has attempted to prevent him from seeing his children by trying to enforce legal 'prohibited steps' orders. She has accused him of all sorts of terrible misdemeanours that she cannot substantiate, which are designed to prevent him from seeing his children. Although they clearly will not succeed in the long run, it is hugely stressful for him, not least because it is costing him vast sums of money to defend himself. He is actively pursuing 'joint residency' so that he can spend as much time as possible with his children, to whom he is clearly devoted.

Ben's 'On the Cards' Realization
When his mother-in-law told his wife she should divorce him – and she agreed and appointed a solicitor…

Ben's 'Light Bulb' Moment
When his wife told him that she had already told the children that they were going to get a divorce – even though they had not yet decided to do it between themselves.

Ben's Advice
Don't let anyone prevent you from seeing your children – however hard the battle and whatever it costs.

MARK

Background
The story of Mark's relationship is one of the most extreme we have heard. He has been divorced for just over a year. He has three grown-up children from the twenty-year marriage. He still lives in the matrimonial home but has had to mortgage it to the hilt in order to pay his ex-wife's divorce settlement. Despite the fact that his home is also his business premises, he will have to sell it soon in order to pay off all his debts from the divorce.

According to Mark, his wife had an addictive personality and she used to drink heavily. Despite her tiny frame she used to consume at least two bottles of wine every single night. He used to have to 'scrape her off the floor' and put her to bed most nights. She regularly checked herself into rehabilitation clinics but nothing seemed to have any effect on her compulsive addictive personality. It has only been in the very short time since he has been divorced that Mark has finally realized how dysfunctional his marriage was and the devastating effect it has had not only on him but on his children.

His ex-wife demonstrated all the classic signs of narcissism during their marriage. She was self-obsessed and needed constant attention, even when it was completely inappropriate. For example, when her sister committed suicide she seemed to derive a real 'high' from the ensuing attention received from concerned friends and family and when she gave an address at the funeral it was almost as though she were playing a 'starring role' in a TV drama.

In addition to her alcohol problem she was also a sex-addict. Mark discovered towards the end of their relationship that almost throughout the entire marriage she had conducted numerous affairs and one-night stands. She regularly picked up men in bars and had sex with them. Because she did not work and her husband gave her 'everything' she asked for, she was increasingly demanding and after ten years of marriage she insisted that she needed a second home in London. Shortly after they purchased a flat, Mark discovered that she had a married lover who was living with her in London in the second home that he had bought for her.

He later discovered that she had made passes at many of his married friends and he says that he lost many close friends as a result because they were so embarrassed. She had an affair with his father's business partner and used *his* friends to facilitate all the lying and cheating that went with the affair. She totally betrayed him and even after discovering the final affair, Mark gave her more than he needed to in the divorce settlement so that he was able to have a 'clean break' and walk away from the relationship as quickly as possible. Even after the divorce his ex-wife continually contacted him to seek his attention and when he refused to have any more dealings with her, she became increasingly unhinged and abusive.

She used to play sadistic psychological games with him and ultimately Mark realized that she was never going to change. He obtained the quickest divorce possible in a bid to walk away as speedily as possible. Mark says he will find it very hard to trust another woman again.

Mark's 'On the Cards' Realization
When he found out that his wife was having an affair with his father's business partner.

Mark's 'Light Bulb' Moment
When Mark's son told him that his mother had picked a man up in a bar in London and had slept with him whilst her teenage son was also staying there. When she told the children that they were getting a divorce, she delivered the news with a smirk on her face.

Mark's Advice
Be very wary of solicitors! They *can* add an enormous amount of heartache to an already devastating situation by 'ramping up the emotions' and playing each party off against the other. Mediation did work for him but only because the solicitors realized that they had decided on a very quick divorce.

FROM AN OLDER WOMAN'S PERSPECTIVE

LIZZIE

Background

Lizzie is in her mid-seventies and has been married twice but has lived in a long-term relationship as if married three times. Her partner of twenty years, to whom she was devoted, died several years ago. She lives on her own in the Welsh borders. She has three grown-up girls and 'quantities' of grand-children.

Lizzie met her first husband, a doctor, in a shop. She was choosing wool for a sweater that she was going to knit for her then boyfriend. He asked whether she would knit a jersey for him, took her telephone number and the rest is history . . .

According to Lizzie, he was exceptionally charismatic, talented and charming. But he had a terrible temper and a violent streak. When, almost out of desperation, she fell in love with his best friend, her husband attacked her lover and, as a result, he spent almost a year in hospital. Her husband pursued custody of their children and used the fact that she had been 'unfaithful' as a reason for trying to prevent her from seeing her children even though he had been extremely abusive. This was in the days before domestic violence was ever publicly acknowledged. He did not succeed with his custody battle but Lizzie was forced to flee to her mother's home with her three children.

Eventually Lizzie met someone new and remarried, despite suffering a severe attack of cold feet in the run-up to the wedding. The relationship lacked passion and she admits that she felt obliged to marry again in order to provide her children with a stable home and a decent lifestyle that she could not have provided on her own. The marriage lasted a year.

Lizzie's 'On the Cards' Moment
The first time her husband was violent to her.

Lizzie's 'Light Bulb' Moment
When she had to move away to stay with her mother to protect herself and her children.

Lizzie's Advice
1. Don't marry for anything except love – wait for it to come along and hit you between the eyes.
2. Always make sure that you have your own money if possible so that you are financially independent and do not have to rely on a man for your or your children's survival.
3. Beware the children of your ex-partners in court – if you are left money in his will they can become acquisitive, vindictive and vengeful.

JOANNA

Background
Joanna is seventy-five and has recently divorced. She has moved into a new home on her own on the outskirts of a small market town. Whilst in her early thirties and happily married to her first husband, both he and her mother were killed in a tragic car crash and she was left to bring up her three young children on her own. Many years later she married her second husband who had been married twice before.

Joanna asked to be interviewed for this book because

she believes that there is nothing on the market to advise older women going through a divorce. In your seventies you might expect to be widowed – but not to be getting divorced. She thinks that the ensuing turbulent emotions are worse than any bereavement – because she still loves her husband and he is still alive. Their close-knit social circle has been split down the middle by divided loyalties and has caused all manner of upheaval and upset. Joanna has experienced both bereavement and divorce, so is well qualified to make the comparison.

Joanna was married for eighteen years. As a woman born into a more traditional generation, she grew up believing that there was a lot of stigma attached to divorce and also felt that it wasn't quite 'proper' for a woman to involve herself with financial matters or to ask for something – which is why the divorce settlement negotiation was so difficult and painful for her.

It is almost beyond belief, but it seems that the divorce came about because his daughters suggested that they should get divorced! Joanna had always had a very difficult relationship with his grown-up daughters and they had continually interfered in her relationship. They had created tensions and conflict between her and her husband for years – with a constant toxic mix of lies, twisting facts and character assassination – and they succeeded in playing each off against the other in some vicious confrontations. As there was a large amount of real estate involved in the settlement, it was very complicated and even after the divorce his daughters have been continually dragging her back through the courts in order to try to claw back assets that she has already been awarded.

On top of the grief and upheaval that Joanna has

suffered during the separation, she now faces potentially many years of legal disputes in order to protect her interests from his children. It is clearly a terrible way to spend one's retirement. She is stressed, depressed and exhausted.

Joanna's 'On the Cards' Moment
When her husband said that his daughter manipulatively had told him that *she*, Joanne, wanted a divorce.

Joanna's 'Light Bulb' Moment
When her husband wouldn't listen to or believe her and instead allowed himself to be manipulated by his daughters, which ultimately ended in the breakdown of the marriage.

Joanna's Advice
1. Find yourself a 'Rottweiler' of a solicitor! Older women need extra protection – especially from the children of the man they are divorcing.
2. Don't be naïve and don't accept less than you know you should just for the sake of a 'quick and amicable' divorce. There is no such thing and you won't be able to go back for a second bite…

FROM A CHILD'S PERSPECTIVE

We were offered the extraordinary opportunity to interview a pair of non-identical twin sisters aged twenty-one. Both were brought up in the same environment but have very different perspectives and reactions to their parents' divorce, which happened whilst they were at school.

JESS

Background

Jess is an incredibly attractive, poised, insightful young woman and is currently reading European Studies at the University of Exeter. The divorce hit her very hard. At the age of eleven she developed anorexia and battled with it for two years. According to Jess, her anorexia came about as a direct result of her father teasing her for being 'chubby' when she clearly wasn't. In her bid to gain her father's approval, she started dieting and eventually was unable to stop. Her relationship with her father is clearly pivotal to the way that Jess handled her parents' divorce. Once close to him, his alcoholism and the way in which she perceived he treated her mother resulted in an almost total collapse of their relationship post-divorce. She says that she has 'no trust' in him because he repeatedly promised to give up drink and treat her mother better but continually reneged on both. Her father was ex-forces and clearly a member of the 'stiff-upper-lip' brigade. She said she never had any emotional support from him and that he was incapable of showing his feelings.

Jess was recently admitted to hospital suffering from severe depression and is on a cocktail of anti-depressants. She is repeating a year at university because she has missed so much. She still suffers from panic attacks and is frightened of being in public places (such as in lectures) because she fears that she will start crying and be unable to stop herself. As a result of her Cognitive Behavioural Therapy (CBT), Jess has been able to pinpoint the underlying cause of her depression and she says that it is because she was forced to suppress her emotions when she was a child.

Her parents' marriage was incredibly turbulent and

so filled with alcohol-fuelled rows that she wished her parents had separated years before they actually did. She can remember seeing her father pushing her mother violently across a room. Her father refuses to acknowledge any part in his daughter's depression and she recently did not speak to him for more than a year.

Two years before her parents separated, they announced that they were going to get divorced. It turned her life upside down. Due to the twins' reaction, their parents decided to call off the divorce. As nothing further was mentioned and life appeared to continue as normal, Jess thought that it was no longer happening and relaxed. When her mother turned up at her boarding school two years later, therefore, to announce that she was divorcing her father, she was absolutely devastated and it felt as though she were going through a second, even more traumatic, family break-up.

Jess's 'On the Cards' Moment
When her parents first jointly announced that they were going to get a divorce.

Jess's 'Light Bulb' Moment
When her mother turned up at her boarding school and announced that she was leaving her father.

Jess's Advice
1. Never think that it is your fault!
2. Try not to take sides and be as detached as you can.

ROSIE

Background
Like her twin sister Jess, Rosie was at boarding school when her mother announced that she was divorcing her father. Although she was brought up in exactly the same home and school environments as her sister, her perspective is a very different one. She is devoted to her father and her mother and says that her parents' divorce has not put her off marriage, although it has made her very wary. When she meets a man she will always think whether she will want to be with him in twenty years' time or if he has any habits or personality traits that are likely to get worse over time. The only obvious difference in her perspective compared to Jess's is that she did not see her father being physically violent to her mother.

Rosie's 'On The Cards' Moment
She could see her mother's pain from an early age. Her father had a long-term girlfriend and she could see how it affected her mother.

Rosie's 'Light Bulb' Moment
Like Jess it was when her mother turned up at her school. It was a terrible shock because she had 'relaxed' and thought that they were going to stay together.

Rosie's Advice
1. Think about the end-product of divorce and not about your own happiness.
2. Think of what will ultimately be in the best interests of the whole family. If your parents are clearly unhappy living together then it is entirely better that they divorce and then you can all move on with your lives.

3. Don't delay and don't stay together in a misguided attempt to be there for your children because they will know that you are not really 'there' – at least not in a 'together sense'. It will hang over them. Either way, it will be painful but bite the bullet so that you all have a chance to get on with a new life as quickly as possible.

FROM A SOLICITOR'S PERSPECTIVE

MATHEW WADDINGTON, FAMILY SOLICITOR

Background
Mathew is forty-one and has worked for Harrison Clark Rickerbys for the past twelve years. He only deals with Family Law, of which 70 per cent are child-related cases and 30 per cent divorce proceedings. He sits on the Law Society's Children's Panel. He is divorced with two children.

Mathew's Advice:
When you file for divorce it throws you into a world of uncertainty, filled with worries about financial security, and frequently people feel betrayed. The worst part is coming to terms with the fact that you now have to share the upbringing of your children. It is a very negative, emotional time and the very best you can hope for is that your clients are emotionally 'neutral'. However, there is no such thing as an amicable divorce. Judges work on a spectrum between white and black with various shades of grey and they easily work out whether or not proposals and agreements are honest or whether they are just tactics. The truth, therefore, is only a perception and the only truths in this world are mathematical.

A bad client is one that is overly emotional, far too principled and not in possession of a sense of proportion. They won't listen to advice and have no medium- or long-term view about their future. Obviously, lawyers are there to advise, and although they will ultimately follow the clients' instructions you must remember that they are a step removed from your situation so they are in a position to see things more clearly. They have seen it all before so don't push up your costs unnecessarily by dragging out proceedings.

Questions you should ask yourself include: why am I taking this course of action? e.g. if you are fighting over contents or assets, use a sense of proportion as to whether the fight is worth it. Solicitors never continue a case in order to drive up their fees and will only continue to act according to your instructions.

It takes time for the mist to clear during divorce and the red mist of anger can descend very fast! Solicitors are not 'yes' people and they will challenge you and give you advice because the legal stuff on its own is pretty straightforward.

Good clients are those who park their emotions. They take advice and they have a more practical attitude towards the process. They will ask the question: what does this mean for me and my children in terms of outcomes, time and cost – at every stage?

Mathew is a collaborative lawyer and passionately believes that this approach to divorce is the best route for most couples, primarily because it is conducted in face-to-face meetings of a more informal nature and is value-driven. To put this in context, the first meeting attended by the parties and their lawyers is called a 'values meeting', which covers how they want to maintain a relationship, bring up the children, holistic financial matters and how to facilitate the best future for the whole family. This does not preclude such things as financial disclosure or other such issues. It is an inquisitorial approach to divorce rather than an adversarial one and he believes that less damage is done.

What do you think is in your child's best interests? Forget about the parents – it's what is in the best interests of the child that counts. Section one of the Children's Act has three key principles against which all children's matters are evaluated: no delay, non-interference and paramountcy.

Children have a 'voice' in the proceedings and in the majority of cases their voice will be heard.

There are several things to avoid where children are concerned:

- Do not punish your ex by using the children.
- Don't bring unnecessary applications. It is seen as manipulative by the courts and it will only cost you in terms of money and reputation.
- Don't believe that you have an automatic right as a parent to have contact with your children. The over-riding factor is the children's right to see both parents.
- Don't 'slag each other off' in respect of child matters as this will be viewed very dimly by solicitors, judges and CAFCASS. Be child-focused throughout every step of the process and, if you can, put yourself in the mind and body of your own child before making any decisions about their future.

FROM A DISTRICT JUDGE'S PERSPECTIVE

JUDGE JAMES

Background

James is fifty-two, and has been a full-time District Judge for six years. Before appointment he was a solicitor in private practice, specializing mainly in property and commercial disputes. Appointment as a judge is by open competition. Like most of the judiciary, he applied to be a part-time judge in his mid-thirties, and then sat two or three days per month for nine years before being appointed to a full-time post. This is pretty typical, although timescales vary. He will remain as a judge for the rest of his working life.

He does the job because he believes in the justice system (it could certainly be improved but, if used correctly, it is a lot better than it's given credit for), enjoys the process of sorting out problems and because he can, occasionally, make a real difference for the better in people's lives.

He is married with three children, two of whom are at university. He enjoys reading, history, sailing, skiing, gardening, riding his motorbike and playing six-a-side football – badly.

Judge James's Advice

We create rituals and traditions to help us through times of change and upheaval; birth, puberty, marriage and death. The relatively modern phenomenon of widely available divorce is no exception. I see the law and the court's role as providing a structured procedure for untangling the lives of two people in a rational and unemotional way. People often misunderstand what the court's role is in divorce: it is *not* generally to allocate blame, punish wrongdoing or decide a winner. These are not criminal proceedings.

A completely clean break is only generally feasible *if* there are no children involved. More likely those two issues – money and children – will tie the two people together for the foreseeable future. The best that anyone can do is to arrive at a fair and pragmatic arrangement for the future as far as those two issues are concerned. Personally, I think it better if the parties can reach an agreement themselves (with the help of the court and other professionals), but otherwise we will impose a solution: that's what we are here for.

Nobody wins in divorce: sometimes assets may be successfully hidden or a parent excluded from their children's lives, but those are not ultimately victories. They come about only after long and vicious battles – sometimes years long – that take a heavy emotional toll on both sides. I have seen parties' physical and mental health and finances destroyed by years of wrangling, often entirely unaware of the price they, and often their children, are paying and will continue to pay for the rest of their lives.

Particularly if there are children, divorce doesn't mean any relationship is completely over – but the old one is gone. It is a fact that I think men are sometimes more ready to accept. It's history. Be strong. You need to create your new life and a relationship with your ex as *you* want the new one to be.

If you can treat the financial wrangling as a cold business transaction, accept that some compromise is inevitable and do a deal early, and arrive at a practical (if not cordial) working arrangement for managing the residence and contact with your children, then you will have done as well as anyone possibly can do.

Index